Simply Delicious

Effortless Recipes for Everyday Enjoyment

GEORGIA DAVIS

The presentation of the information is without contract or any type of guarantee assurance. The trademarks that are used are without any consent, and the publication of the trademark is without permission or backing by the trademark owner. All trademarks and brands within this book are for clarifying purposes only and are the owned by the owners themselves, not affiliated with this document.

Table of Contents

Chapter 1

Introduction

Welcome to Effortless Cooking

Cooking doesn't have to be a daunting task reserved for those with ample time and advanced culinary skills. Effortless cooking is about making smart choices, using simple techniques, and maximizing the flavors of basic ingredients to create delicious meals with minimal effort. The key lies in preparation, organization, and a few clever strategies that can turn anyone into a confident cook.

One of the first steps towards effortless cooking is organizing your kitchen. A well-organized kitchen saves time and reduces stress. Start by arranging your cabinets and pantry so that similar items are grouped together. Spices should be easily accessible, and frequently used utensils should be within reach. Invest in clear containers for dry goods and label them to avoid confusion. This level of organization not only makes cooking more efficient but also more enjoyable.

Another cornerstone of effortless cooking is meal planning. Spend a few minutes each week planning your meals. This doesn't mean you need to stick to a rigid menu, but having a general idea of what you'd like to cook can simplify grocery shopping and ensure that you have all the necessary ingredients on hand. Create a list of versatile recipes that you can rotate through, and make sure to include a mix of proteins, vegetables, and grains.

Batch cooking is a game-changer for those looking to streamline their time in the kitchen. Prepare larger quantities of meals that can be easily reheated throughout the week. Soups, stews, casseroles, and pasta dishes are excellent candidates for batch cooking. Not only does this save time, but it also ensures you always have a homemade meal ready, reducing the temptation to order takeout.

When it comes to cooking techniques, simplicity is your best friend. Master a few basic techniques that can be applied to a variety of dishes. Sautéing, roasting, and grilling are essential methods that can elevate simple ingredients. Sautéing vegetables in olive oil with a pinch of salt and pepper can bring out their natural flavors, while roasting meats and vegetables in the oven allows you to achieve a rich, caramelized exterior with minimal effort. Grilling adds a smoky flavor that can transform even the most basic ingredients into a gourmet experience.

Using high-quality ingredients can make a significant difference in the flavor of your dishes without requiring complicated recipes. Fresh, seasonal produce, good-quality olive oil, and fresh herbs can enhance the taste of your meals. Visit your local farmers' market to find the best produce and support local growers. When you start with great ingredients, you can keep the seasoning simple and still achieve delicious results.

One of the most valuable tips for effortless cooking is learning to make the most of your leftovers. Transforming leftovers into new meals can save time and reduce waste. For instance, roast chicken can be used in salads, sandwiches, or stir-fries. Leftover vegetables can be added to frittatas, soups, or grain bowls. By getting creative with your leftovers, you can enjoy a variety of meals without starting from scratch each time.

Effortless cooking also involves making smart use of kitchen gadgets and appliances. A slow cooker or Instant Pot can be a lifesaver for busy individuals. These appliances allow you to prepare meals with minimal hands-on time. Simply add your ingredients, set the timer, and let the appliance do the work. Slow cookers are perfect for stews, curries, and braised dishes, while an Instant Pot can significantly reduce cooking times for a variety of recipes.

Another great tool for effortless cooking is a high-quality chef's knife. A sharp knife makes chopping and slicing faster and safer. It's worth investing in a good knife and learning how to maintain its sharpness. Proper knife skills can also speed up your prep time and improve the presentation of your dishes.

Effortless cooking doesn't mean sacrificing flavor or creativity. Experiment with different cuisines and flavor profiles to keep your meals interesting. Keep a well-stocked spice rack and don't be afraid to try new spices and herbs. Simple additions like cumin, paprika, or fresh basil can completely transform a dish. Start with small amounts and adjust to your taste preferences.

Time management is another crucial aspect of effortless cooking. Learn to multitask and make the most of your cooking time. For example, while your vegetables are roasting in the oven, you can prepare a salad or cook a pot of rice. By overlapping tasks, you can have multiple components of your meal ready at the same time.

One often-overlooked aspect of effortless cooking is clean-up. A clean workspace makes cooking more enjoyable and less chaotic. Clean as you go to avoid a mountain of dishes at the end of your meal. Wash utensils and cutting boards as soon as you're done using them, and wipe down countertops regularly. This habit not only keeps your kitchen tidy but also makes the cooking process smoother.

Incorporating these strategies into your routine can make cooking feel less like a chore and more like a creative, enjoyable activity. Start small by implementing one or two changes at a time, and gradually build on your successes. Remember that the goal of effortless cooking is to make delicious, homemade meals without stress or complexity. With a bit of planning, organization, and practice, anyone can become an efficient and confident cook. Another factor that contributes to effortless cooking is understanding the importance of mise en place. This French term, meaning "everything in its place," emphasizes the preparation of ingredients before you start cooking. By chopping vegetables, measuring spices, and organizing all necessary components ahead of time, you streamline the cooking process and reduce the chances of missing steps or ingredients. This methodical approach not only saves time but also enhances the overall cooking experience.

The Philosophy of Simple and Delicious

Simple and delicious cooking is less about strict recipes and more about understanding the essence of flavors, ingredients, and techniques. This philosophy champions the idea that great meals don't require complicated steps or exotic ingredients, but rather a thoughtful approach to the basics. By focusing on simplicity and taste, you can create dishes that are both satisfying and stress-free.

The foundation of this philosophy begins with fresh, high-quality ingredients. When you start with the best produce, meats, and pantry staples, you're already halfway to a delicious meal. Fresh ingredients have natural flavors that need minimal enhancement. Visit local farmers' markets where you can find seasonal fruits and vegetables, often harvested at their peak ripeness. Not only does this support local agriculture, but it also ensures that your meals are vibrant and full of flavor.

Understanding the balance and harmony of flavors is another crucial aspect. The interplay between sweet, salty, sour, and umami can turn a simple dish into something extraordinary. For instance, a splash of lemon juice can brighten up a rich, creamy pasta, while a pinch of salt can elevate the sweetness of roasted carrots. Experiment with different combinations to discover what pleases your palate.

One of the most effective ways to achieve simplicity in cooking is to master a few essential techniques. Roasting, for example, is a method that can be applied to a variety of vegetables and proteins. The high heat caramelizes the natural sugars, creating a depth of flavor with minimal effort. Similarly, pan-searing meats can develop a delicious crust while keeping the inside tender and juicy. These techniques are straightforward but yield impressive results.

Herbs and spices are the unsung heroes of simple cooking. Fresh herbs like basil, cilantro, and parsley can add a burst of freshness to any dish. Dried spices such as cumin, paprika, and oregano bring warmth and complexity. Learning how to use these flavor enhancers can transform your cooking. Keep a well-stocked spice rack and don't be afraid to experiment. Start with small amounts and adjust to taste.

A cornerstone of this philosophy is the idea that less is more. Overloading a dish with too many ingredients or flavors can often lead to confusion rather than harmony. Focus on highlighting a few key components and letting them shine. For example, a simple tomato salad with fresh mozzarella, basil, and a drizzle of olive oil can be more satisfying than a complex dish with multiple competing elements.

Cooking with simplicity doesn't mean sacrificing nutritional value. In fact, simple meals often highlight whole, unprocessed foods that are naturally nutritious. Grains like quinoa, farro, and brown rice can serve as the base for many meals, providing fiber and essential nutrients. Pair them with a variety of colorful vegetables and lean proteins for a balanced, wholesome meal.

One practical approach to maintaining simplicity is to use fewer dishes and utensils. One-pot meals, sheet pan dinners, and skillet dishes minimize cleanup and keep the cooking process straightforward. These methods allow flavors to meld together beautifully, often resulting in richer, more cohesive dishes. A hearty vegetable stew or a chicken and rice casserole can be both comforting and easy to prepare.

The philosophy of simple and delicious also embraces the idea of intuition in cooking. Trusting your senses—taste, smell, sight, and touch—can guide you more effectively than any recipe. Taste your food as you cook and adjust seasoning as needed. Pay attention to the aroma of ingredients as they cook; it can tell you if something is browning too quickly or needs more time. The visual cues, like the golden-brown color of roasted vegetables or the bubbling of a simmering sauce, are also invaluable.

Moreover, simplicity in cooking can be achieved by leveraging leftovers creatively. Transform yesterday's dinner into today's lunch with minimal effort. Leftover roasted chicken can be shredded into a salad, or mixed with vegetables for a quick stir-fry. This not only reduces waste but also saves time and energy.

Another important aspect of this philosophy is the joy of sharing meals. Food has always been a medium to bring people together. Simple, delicious dishes can be a focal point of gatherings, fostering connections and creating memories. A well-cooked meal doesn't need to be extravagant to be appreciated. Sharing a homemade pizza or a pot of chili with friends can be just as rewarding as a multi-course dinner.

Mindfulness in cooking is an often-overlooked but vital part of this approach. Being present and engaged in the process can turn cooking into a meditative practice rather than a chore. Take the time to appreciate the textures, colors, and smells of the ingredients. This mindfulness can enhance your enjoyment of cooking and eating, making the entire experience more fulfilling.

Embracing simplicity also means being flexible and adaptive. Cooking doesn't always go as planned, and that's okay. If you run out of an ingredient, think creatively about substitutes. Maybe you can use yogurt instead of sour cream, or swap spinach for kale. This adaptability not only makes cooking less stressful but also more fun.

To truly embody the philosophy of simple and delicious, it's important to continue learning and evolving. Explore different cuisines and cooking styles. Each culture has its own approach to simplicity and flavor that can inspire your cooking. For instance, Italian cuisine often focuses on a few high-quality ingredients prepared with care, while Japanese cuisine emphasizes balance and harmony in flavors.

Ultimately, the philosophy of simple and delicious cooking is about creating meals that nourish both body and soul. It's about finding joy in the process and satisfaction in the results. By focusing on quality ingredients, mastering basic techniques, and embracing a minimalist approach, you can create dishes that are not only easy to make but also delightful to eat. This approach to cooking brings a sense of ease and pleasure to your kitchen, making every meal a celebration of simplicity and taste. Incorporating seasonal ingredients into your cooking is another hallmark of the simple and delicious philosophy. Seasonal produce is often fresher, more flavorful, and more affordable. It also encourages variety in your diet, as different fruits and vegetables come into season throughout the year. In the winter, you might focus on root vegetables and hearty greens, while summer can be a celebration of tomatoes, zucchini, and berries. Let the changing seasons guide your meal planning and enjoy the natural rhythm of the harvest.

Essential Tools and Ingredients

A well-equipped kitchen is the cornerstone of successful cooking. The right tools and ingredients not only make the cooking process more efficient but also elevate the quality of your dishes. Whether you're a novice or a seasoned cook, understanding the essentials can transform your culinary experience.

First and foremost, a good chef's knife is indispensable. This versatile tool is used for chopping, slicing, dicing, and mincing. Invest in a high-quality knife that feels comfortable in your hand. Regularly sharpen it to maintain its efficiency and safety. A sharp knife not only makes your work easier but also reduces the risk of accidents.

A sturdy cutting board is equally important. Wooden or bamboo boards are preferred because they are gentle on knives and have natural antimicrobial properties. Ensure your cutting board is large enough to handle big tasks but not so large that it becomes cumbersome.

Measuring cups and spoons are fundamental for accurate cooking and baking. Even seasoned cooks who rely on intuition for seasoning and flavoring need these tools for precise measurements, especially in baking, where accuracy is crucial. Having a set of dry and liquid measuring cups, along with a range of measuring spoons, ensures you can follow recipes accurately.

Mixing bowls of various sizes are another must-have. They are used for everything from mixing ingredients to serving salads. Stainless steel bowls are durable and versatile, suitable for a variety of tasks, including marinating, mixing, and even heating over a double boiler.

A set of high-quality pots and pans is essential. Start with a non-stick skillet, a stainless steel sauté pan, and a cast-iron skillet. Non-stick skillets are perfect for delicate tasks like cooking eggs or pancakes, while stainless steel pans are ideal for searing meats and making pan sauces. Cast-iron skillets are incredibly versatile, retaining heat well and transitioning seamlessly from stovetop to oven.

Baking sheets, also known as sheet pans, are indispensable for roasting vegetables, baking cookies, and more. Look for heavy-duty, rimmed baking sheets that won't warp under high heat. Pair them with silicone baking mats or parchment paper to prevent sticking and make cleanup easier.

A Dutch oven is another versatile tool. This heavy, enameled cast iron pot is perfect for slow-cooking, braising, and making soups and stews. Its ability to maintain consistent heat makes it ideal for long-cooking dishes that develop deep flavors over time.

A food processor can save you a lot of time and effort. This multi-functional appliance can chop, slice, grate, and even knead dough. It's particularly useful for making sauces, dips, and purees. While a blender can handle many of these tasks, a food processor is better suited for thicker mixtures and more precise cuts.

Tongs, spatulas, and wooden spoons are basic tools you'll use daily. Tongs are perfect for flipping meat, tossing salads, and removing items from hot water. Look for ones with a good grip and a locking mechanism for easy storage. Silicone spatulas are heat-resistant and ideal for scraping bowls and pans. Wooden spoons are durable and won't scratch your cookware, making them perfect for stirring and mixing.

A kitchen scale is an often overlooked but incredibly useful tool. It ensures precise measurements, especially in baking where weight is more accurate than volume. It also helps with portion control and can be used to measure ingredients for recipes that require exact quantities.

Colanders and sieves are necessary for draining pasta, rinsing vegetables, and sifting flour. A large colander with sturdy handles and a stable base is ideal for draining large quantities. A fine-mesh sieve is perfect for tasks that require more precision, like straining sauces or sifting dry ingredients.

A pair of kitchen shears is another versatile tool. They can be used for a variety of tasks, from snipping herbs to cutting poultry. Look for shears that come apart for easy cleaning, as this ensures they remain hygienic.

Now, let's talk about essential ingredients. Salt is the foundation of flavor. Kosher salt and sea salt are preferred by many chefs for their purity and texture. They dissolve easily and enhance the natural flavors of your ingredients. Keep a container of flaky sea salt for finishing dishes, adding a burst of flavor and a pleasing crunch.

Olive oil is another kitchen staple. Extra-virgin olive oil is perfect for salads, dipping bread, and finishing dishes, while regular olive oil is suitable for cooking. Its rich flavor and health benefits make it a versatile and valuable ingredient.

Vinegars, such as balsamic, red wine, and apple cider, add acidity and brightness to your dishes. They are essential for making dressings, marinades, and sauces. Each type of vinegar offers a unique flavor profile, so it's worth having a variety on hand.

Garlic and onions are the backbone of many savory dishes. Fresh garlic cloves and a variety of onions—yellow, red, and shallots—are indispensable for adding depth and complexity to your cooking. Store them in a cool, dry place to keep them fresh longer.

Herbs and spices are crucial for flavoring your food. Fresh herbs like basil, cilantro, and parsley can elevate a dish with their vibrant flavors. Dried herbs and spices, including thyme, oregano, cumin, and paprika, are also essential. Store them in a cool, dark place to preserve their potency.

Canned tomatoes are a pantry staple. They are versatile and can be used in a variety of dishes, from sauces and soups to stews and braises. Look for whole, crushed, and diced tomatoes to suit different recipes.

A selection of grains and legumes, such as rice, quinoa, lentils, and beans, provides a foundation for many meals. These ingredients are not only nutritious but also versatile, serving as the base for salads, soups, and main dishes. Keep a variety of these staples in your pantry to ensure you always have the makings of a hearty meal.

Stock and broth are essential for adding depth to soups, stews, and sauces. While homemade stock is always preferable, high-quality store-bought options are a convenient alternative. Chicken, beef, and vegetable broths are the most common, each bringing unique flavors to your dishes.

Dairy products like butter, milk, and cheese are fundamental ingredients. Butter adds richness and flavor, while milk and cream are essential for baking and making sauces. A variety of cheeses, such as Parmesan, cheddar, and mozzarella, can enhance many dishes with their distinct flavors and textures.

Eggs are incredibly versatile and a staple in both savory and sweet recipes. They can be used in everything from baking to making sauces, or enjoyed on their own as a simple meal. Keep a dozen eggs in your fridge to ensure you have this versatile ingredient on hand.

By equipping your kitchen with these essential tools and ingredients, you'll be prepared to tackle a wide range of recipes and cooking techniques. Investing in quality tools and keeping a well-stocked pantry not only makes cooking more enjoyable but also ensures that you can create delicious, wholesome meals with ease. Whether you're preparing a simple weeknight dinner or an elaborate feast, these essentials will serve as the foundation of your culinary adventures. In addition to these core tools and ingredients, there are a few more items that can significantly enhance your cooking experience. Having a reliable set of kitchen timers and thermometers is crucial for precision. An instant-read thermometer ensures meats and baked goods are cooked to the correct temperature, eliminating guesswork and enhancing food safety. A timer helps keep track of cooking times, preventing overcooking or burning.

Tips for Efficient Cooking

Cooking can be a delightful and rewarding experience, but it can also be time-consuming and stressful if not approached efficiently. Whether you're preparing a quick weeknight dinner or an elaborate feast, mastering the art of efficient cooking can save you time, reduce stress, and make the process more enjoyable. Here are some tips to help you streamline your kitchen routine and become a more efficient cook.

One of the most effective ways to improve your cooking efficiency is through meal planning. By taking the time to plan your meals for the week, you can ensure that you have all the necessary ingredients on hand, reducing the need for last-minute grocery runs. Start by creating a menu for the week, taking into account your schedule and any special dietary requirements. Once you have your menu, make a detailed shopping list organized by section of the grocery store. This not only saves time while shopping but also helps prevent impulse buys.

Another key aspect of efficient cooking is proper mise en place, a French term that means "everything in its place." Before you start cooking, gather all your ingredients and tools, and prepare them as needed. This might include washing and chopping vegetables, measuring out spices, and preheating your oven. By having everything ready to go, you can move smoothly through the cooking process without having to stop and search for ingredients or equipment.

Batch cooking is another powerful strategy for efficient cooking. By preparing larger quantities of food at once, you can save time later in the week. For example, cook a large pot of rice or quinoa, roast a tray of vegetables, or make a big batch of soup or stew. These can be stored in the fridge or freezer and used as the base for multiple meals. Not only does this save time, but it also ensures you always have healthy, homemade options available.

Using the right tools can also significantly boost your cooking efficiency. Invest in a few high-quality kitchen appliances, such as a slow cooker, pressure cooker, or food processor. These tools can save you time and effort by handling tasks like chopping, blending, and slow-cooking. For instance, a slow cooker allows you to prepare meals in the morning and have them ready by dinner time with minimal hands-on effort. A pressure cooker can drastically reduce cooking times for dishes like beans, stews, and braised meats.

Keeping your kitchen organized is essential for efficient cooking. Make sure your frequently used tools and ingredients are easily accessible. Arrange your pantry, fridge, and cabinets in a way that makes sense to you, grouping similar items together. Labeling containers and shelves can also help you quickly find what you need. An organized kitchen reduces the time spent searching for items and helps maintain a smooth workflow.

Multitasking wisely can also enhance your cooking efficiency. While some tasks require your full attention, others can be done simultaneously. For example, while waiting for water to boil or the oven to preheat, you can chop vegetables or prepare a salad. However, be mindful not to take on too many tasks at once, as this can lead to mistakes or accidents. Focus on combining tasks that complement each other and can be done safely.

Learning to use your knife skills efficiently can save you a significant amount of time. Practicing basic techniques like slicing, dicing, and chopping can make food preparation faster and more enjoyable. A sharp knife is crucial for efficient cutting, so make sure to keep your knives well-maintained. Additionally, using a proper cutting board and employing the right techniques can help prevent injuries and ensure consistent results.

Streamlining your cleanup process can also make cooking more efficient. Clean as you go by washing dishes, wiping counters, and putting away ingredients as you use them. This prevents a large pile of dishes from accumulating and makes the final cleanup faster and less daunting. Consider using a garbage bowl or compost bin on your countertop to collect food scraps as you work, reducing trips to the trash can.

Cooking in larger quantities and freezing portions for later use is another excellent efficiency tip. Many dishes, such as casseroles, soups, and sauces, freeze well and can be reheated for quick meals. By doubling recipes and freezing half, you can build a stockpile of homemade meals that are ready to go on busy days. Be sure to label and date your frozen items to keep track of what you have and use older items first.

Embracing shortcuts and convenience items when appropriate can also save time without sacrificing quality. Pre-cut vegetables, canned beans, and store-bought sauces can be great time-savers. While it's important to be mindful of nutritional content and avoid overly processed items, these shortcuts can be valuable tools in your efficiency toolkit. For example, using pre-washed salad greens or frozen vegetables can significantly cut down on prep time.

Another tip for efficient cooking is to master a few versatile recipes that can be easily adapted to different ingredients. For example, a basic stir-fry or frittata recipe can be customized with whatever vegetables, proteins, and seasonings you have on hand. This flexibility allows you to make the most of your ingredients and reduce food waste. Having a repertoire of go-to recipes that you can whip up quickly with minimal fuss can be a lifesaver on busy nights.

Finally, don't be afraid to enlist help when cooking. If you have family members or roommates, involve them in the process. Assign tasks based on skill level and interest, and work together to prepare meals. Not only does this make cooking more efficient, but it can also be a fun and collaborative experience. Teaching children basic cooking skills, for example, not only helps you but also equips them with valuable life skills.

Efficient cooking is about more than just saving time; it's about creating a kitchen environment that allows you to enjoy the process and produce delicious, homemade meals with ease. By incorporating these tips into your routine, you can streamline your workflow, reduce stress, and make the most of your time in the kitchen. With practice and a little planning, you'll find that efficient cooking becomes second nature, allowing you to focus on the joy of creating and sharing good food. Efficient cooking also involves being mindful of your energy and resources. Utilizing energy-efficient appliances and cooking methods can help you save both time and money. For instance, using a microwave or an induction cooktop can be more energy-efficient than traditional stovetops or ovens. These appliances often cook food faster, which not only saves time but also reduces energy consumption. Additionally, cooking with lids on pots and pans can speed up cooking times and conserve energy by retaining heat.

How to Use This Book

Understanding how to make the most out of this book will significantly enhance your learning experience and help you apply the knowledge effectively. This book is designed to be a comprehensive guide, providing you with practical advice, detailed explanations, and actionable strategies to master the subject. To fully benefit from the content, it's essential to approach it with a clear strategy and an open mind, ready to absorb and implement new ideas.

Begin your journey by familiarizing yourself with the table of contents. The table of contents is your roadmap, offering a structured overview of the topics covered. Take a moment to skim through it and identify the chapters that immediately catch your interest. This will give you a sense of what to expect and help you prioritize the areas you want to focus on first. While the book is designed to be read sequentially, feel free to jump to sections that are most relevant to your current needs or questions.

As you start reading, keep a notebook or digital document handy. Jot down key points, take notes on concepts that resonate with you, and write questions or thoughts that arise. This practice not only reinforces your understanding but also creates a personalized reference you can revisit later. Highlighting important passages directly in the book can also be helpful, especially if you plan to refer back to specific sections.

Engage actively with the content by reflecting on how it applies to your own experiences or challenges. Whenever you encounter a new concept or strategy, think about how you can implement it in your daily life or work. For instance, if a chapter discusses time management techniques, consider how you can integrate those techniques into your routine. Real-world application is crucial for internalizing and benefiting from the material.

Each chapter is designed with a balance of theory and practical advice. Pay close attention to the examples and case studies provided. These are not just illustrative; they are meant to show you how the principles discussed can be applied in various contexts. Analyzing these examples can provide deeper insights and help you see the practical implications of the concepts.

Don't rush through the book. Take your time to digest each chapter thoroughly before moving on to the next. Allow yourself the space to fully understand and reflect on the information presented. Sometimes, stepping away from the book for a brief period can help consolidate your learning. When you return, you may find that concepts are clearer and connections between ideas are more apparent.

Discussion and collaboration can greatly enhance your understanding of the material. If possible, form a study group or find a reading partner who is also interested in the topic. Discussing chapters, sharing insights, and debating different viewpoints can deepen your comprehension and expose you to perspectives you might not have considered. This collaborative approach can make the learning process more engaging and enjoyable.

Many chapters include exercises or activities designed to reinforce the material. Don't skip these. Engaging with the exercises can help you practice and apply what you've learned, solidifying your grasp of the concepts. Treat these activities as opportunities to test your understanding and identify areas where you might need further clarification.

Consider setting specific goals for what you want to achieve with this book. Whether it's mastering a particular skill, gaining a deeper understanding of a subject, or solving a specific problem, having clear objectives can guide your reading and keep you motivated. Periodically review your goals to see how far you've come and adjust them as needed based on your progress and evolving interests.

As you work through the book, be open to adjusting your approach based on what works best for you. Everyone learns differently, and it's important to find a method that suits your style. Some readers may benefit from taking detailed notes, while others might prefer summarizing each chapter in their own words. Experiment with different techniques to discover what helps you retain and apply the information most effectively.

Revisiting chapters after some time has passed can be incredibly beneficial. Re-reading sections can reinforce your understanding and reveal nuances you might have missed during the first read. It's also a good way to refresh your memory on key points and ensure that the material remains relevant and useful to you.

Beyond reading, consider how you can integrate the insights from this book into your ongoing personal and professional development. Identify resources, such as other books, articles, courses, or experts, that can further expand your knowledge on specific topics of interest. This approach will help you build a more comprehensive understanding and keep you engaged with the subject matter long after you've finished this book.

Finally, don't hesitate to provide feedback on the book. Sharing your thoughts, questions, and suggestions can help improve future editions and provide valuable insights for other readers. Whether through reviews, discussion forums, or direct communication with the author, your input can contribute to a richer, more effective learning resource for everyone.

By approaching this book with a strategic and engaged mindset, you can maximize its benefits and turn the knowledge within into practical, actionable wisdom. Happy reading! Remember, this book is a tool designed to help you grow and achieve your goals. Your active participation and commitment to applying the concepts will determine how much you gain from it. Here are a few additional strategies to help you make the most out of your reading experience.

Chapter 2

Quick Breakfasts

Energizing Smoothies

Nothing beats the refreshing, nutrient-packed power of a well-crafted smoothie to kickstart your day or recharge your energy levels after a workout. Energizing smoothies are not just delicious; they are also a convenient way to ensure you're getting a variety of vitamins, minerals, and other essential nutrients. This chapter delves into the art and science of creating smoothies that not only taste great but also provide a significant energy boost to keep you going throughout the day.

The foundation of an energizing smoothie lies in selecting the right ingredients. Fresh fruits like bananas, berries, and mangoes are excellent starting points. Bananas, for instance, are rich in potassium and natural sugars, which provide a quick energy release. Berries, on the other hand, are packed with antioxidants and fiber, promoting sustained energy levels and overall health. Mangoes add a tropical flavor while offering a good dose of vitamins A and C, which are crucial for maintaining energy and boosting the immune system.

To enhance the nutritional profile of your smoothie, consider adding leafy greens such as spinach or kale. These greens are low in calories but high in essential nutrients like iron, calcium, and magnesium. Iron is particularly important for energy production as it helps in the formation of hemoglobin, which transports oxygen to your cells. Magnesium plays a vital role in over 300 biochemical reactions in the body, including energy production.

Protein is another key component of an energizing smoothie. It helps in muscle repair and growth, keeps you feeling full longer, and stabilizes blood sugar levels, preventing energy crashes. There are various ways to incorporate protein into your smoothie. Greek yogurt is a popular choice, offering a creamy texture and a substantial protein boost. For a plant-based option, consider adding a scoop of protein powder made from peas, hemp, or brown rice. Nut butters like almond or peanut butter are also excellent additions, providing both protein and healthy fats.

Healthy fats are essential for sustained energy. They slow down the digestion of carbohydrates, leading to a gradual release of energy rather than a quick spike followed by a crash. Avocado is a fantastic source of healthy fats and adds a creamy texture to your smoothie. Alternatively, you can add a tablespoon of chia seeds or flaxseeds. These seeds are not only rich in omega-3 fatty acids but also provide fiber, which aids in digestion and keeps you feeling satisfied.

Hydration is another crucial aspect of maintaining energy levels. Coconut water is an excellent base for your smoothie as it contains electrolytes like potassium, sodium, and magnesium, which help maintain fluid balance and prevent dehydration. Almond milk or any other plant-based milk can also be used as a base, adding a subtle flavor and additional nutrients.

To further boost the energy quotient of your smoothie, consider adding superfoods. Spirulina, a blue-green algae, is packed with protein, vitamins, and minerals, and has been shown to improve endurance and reduce fatigue. Maca powder, derived from a Peruvian root, is known for its energy-enhancing properties and ability to balance hormones. A small amount of matcha powder can also provide a gentle caffeine boost along with antioxidants.

Creating a perfect energizing smoothie is as much about the process as it is about the ingredients. Start by adding your liquid base to the blender to ensure a smooth blending process. Follow with leafy greens, then fruits, and finally, your protein sources and superfoods. Blending in this order helps achieve a consistent texture and ensures all ingredients are well incorporated.

Experimentation is key to finding your favorite smoothie combinations. Don't be afraid to mix and match different fruits, greens, and superfoods to discover what works best for your taste and energy needs. A classic combination to try is a green smoothie made with spinach, banana, mango, Greek yogurt, and a tablespoon of chia seeds. For a berry boost, blend together strawberries, blueberries, a handful of kale, almond milk, and a scoop of protein powder.

Consistency and balance are vital for reaping the full benefits of energizing smoothies. While it might be tempting to load your smoothie with all your favorite ingredients, keeping a balance between fruits, vegetables, proteins, and fats ensures you're not overloading on sugars or missing out on essential nutrients. Aim for a mix that includes a variety of colors and food groups to cover a broad spectrum of vitamins and minerals.

Incorporating energizing smoothies into your daily routine can be transformative. Start your day with a smoothie to jumpstart your metabolism and provide a steady stream of energy. Post-workout smoothies can aid in recovery and replenish your energy stores. Even as a midday snack, a well-balanced smoothie can prevent the afternoon slump and keep you focused and productive.

Mindfulness in preparation and consumption can also enhance the benefits of your smoothies. Take a moment to enjoy the process of selecting ingredients, blending them, and savoring each sip. This mindfulness can make the act of drinking a smoothie a ritual that not only nourishes your body but also calms your mind and prepares you for the day ahead.

Finally, pay attention to how different smoothies affect your energy levels and overall well-being. Everyone's body is unique, and what works for one person might not work for another. Keep a journal of your smoothie ingredients and note how you feel after consuming them. This practice can help you identify the combinations that best suit your energy needs and taste preferences.

By focusing on the right ingredients, balancing your nutrients, and paying attention to your body's responses, you can master the art of creating energizing smoothies. These nutrient-dense drinks can become a cornerstone of your healthy lifestyle, providing you with the sustained energy and vitality needed to tackle your daily challenges. Enjoy the journey of exploring new flavors and combinations, and relish the boost of energy that comes with each delicious sip. Remember to keep your smoothies varied and seasonal to maximize freshness and nutrient content. Seasonal fruits and vegetables are often more flavorful and nutritious, as they are harvested at their peak. In the summer, enjoy the abundance of berries, peaches, and leafy greens. Come fall, incorporate apples, pumpkins, and hearty greens like kale. Winter might bring citrus fruits, persimmons, and root vegetables, while spring offers a plethora of berries, fresh greens, and tropical fruits.

Easy Overnight Oats

Imagine waking up to a nutritious, delicious breakfast that's ready to eat and requires no morning prep. Welcome to the world of easy overnight oats. This simple yet versatile dish can transform your mornings, providing a hearty meal that keeps you full and energized throughout the day. Overnight oats are not only convenient but also packed with nutrients, making them a favorite among busy individuals and health enthusiasts alike.

At its core, overnight oats are made by soaking rolled oats in liquid overnight. This process softens the oats, eliminating the need for cooking. The basic recipe is straightforward: combine equal parts oats and your choice of liquid, let them sit in the refrigerator overnight, and enjoy them cold or warm the next morning. The beauty of overnight oats lies in their flexibility. You can tailor the ingredients to suit your taste preferences and nutritional needs.

Start with high-quality oats. Rolled oats are the best choice for overnight oats because they soften perfectly without becoming mushy. Steel-cut oats can be used if you prefer a chewier texture, but they require a bit more liquid and a longer soaking time. Instant oats, however, tend to become too mushy and are generally not recommended.

Choosing the right liquid is crucial for achieving the desired consistency and flavor. Milk is a popular choice, providing a creamy texture and additional protein. Dairy alternatives such as almond milk, soy milk, or oat milk work just as well and cater to those who are lactose intolerant or prefer a plant-based diet. For a richer flavor, you might consider using coconut milk. Water can also be used, though it results in a less creamy texture.

To add sweetness and flavor, consider incorporating natural sweeteners and spices. Honey, maple syrup, or agave nectar are excellent choices for a touch of sweetness. Spices like cinnamon, nutmeg, or vanilla extract can elevate the flavor profile, making your oats more enjoyable. Remember, a little goes a long way, so start with small amounts and adjust to taste.

One of the joys of overnight oats is the endless variety of mix-ins and toppings you can experiment with. Fresh or dried fruits add natural sweetness and a burst of flavor. Berries, bananas, apples, and mangoes are popular choices. For added texture and nutrition, consider nuts and seeds such as almonds, walnuts, chia seeds, or flaxseeds. Nut butters like peanut butter or almond butter not only add creaminess but also boost the protein content.

For those looking to increase their fiber intake, adding a tablespoon of chia seeds or flaxseeds can make a significant difference. Both are rich in omega-3 fatty acids and fiber, promoting heart health and aiding digestion. Chia seeds also absorb liquid and expand, helping to thicken the oats and create a pudding-like consistency.

Yogurt is another fantastic addition to overnight oats. Greek yogurt, in particular, adds a creamy texture and a substantial protein boost. It also introduces probiotics, which are beneficial for gut health. If you prefer a dairy-free option, coconut yogurt or almond milk yogurt are great alternatives.

The preparation process for overnight oats is incredibly simple. Begin by combining your oats and liquid in a jar or container with a lid. Add your chosen sweeteners and spices, then mix in any fruits, nuts, seeds, or yogurt. Stir well to ensure all ingredients are evenly distributed. Seal the container and place it in the refrigerator overnight, or for at least 4-6 hours. The oats will absorb the liquid and soften, creating a ready-to-eat breakfast by morning.

For those who enjoy variety, making multiple jars of different flavors can keep breakfast exciting throughout the week. Here are a few flavor ideas to get you started:

1. **Classic Vanilla and Berry**: Combine oats with almond milk, a splash of vanilla extract,

and a handful of mixed berries. Sweeten with a drizzle of honey.

2. **Peanut Butter Banana**: Mix oats with milk, a spoonful of peanut butter, and sliced banana. Add a pinch of cinnamon for extra warmth.

3. **Apple Cinnamon**: Use oats, milk, diced apple, cinnamon, and a touch of maple syrup. Add a handful of walnuts for crunch.

4. **Chocolate Almond**: Blend oats with chocolate almond milk, a spoonful of almond butter, and a sprinkle of cocoa powder. Top with sliced almonds.

5. **Tropical Paradise**: Combine oats with coconut milk, diced mango, pineapple chunks, and a sprinkle of shredded coconut.

Experimenting with different combinations can help you discover your favorite flavors and keep breakfast enjoyable. Additionally, overnight oats can be a great way to use up leftover fruits or nuts in your pantry.

Overnight oats are not only a time-saver but also a nutritional powerhouse. Oats are rich in soluble fiber, particularly beta-glucan, which helps lower cholesterol levels and improves heart health. They provide a steady release of energy, keeping you full and satisfied until your next meal. Pairing oats with protein-rich ingredients like yogurt or nuts can further enhance their satiating effect.

Including fruits and nuts in your oats adds vitamins, minerals, and antioxidants to your diet. Berries, for instance, are high in vitamin C and antioxidants, which help combat inflammation and protect against chronic diseases. Nuts and seeds provide healthy fats, essential for brain function and overall health.

For those managing blood sugar levels, overnight oats can be a beneficial choice. The fiber in oats slows down the absorption of sugar, preventing spikes in blood glucose. Opting for low-glycemic fruits like berries and adding protein sources can further stabilize blood sugar levels.

Incorporating overnight oats into your routine can also support weight management. The combination of fiber, protein, and healthy fats helps control appetite and reduce unhealthy snacking. By preparing your oats in advance, you're less likely to skip breakfast or resort to less nutritious options.

Beyond their health benefits, overnight oats are environmentally friendly. Preparing them at home reduces reliance on single-use packaging often associated with store-bought breakfast items. Using reusable containers for your oats is a small but meaningful step towards reducing waste.

In summary, easy overnight oats offer a perfect blend of convenience, nutrition, and versatility. By selecting high-quality ingredients and experimenting with flavors, you can create a breakfast that suits your taste and nutritional needs. Whether you're a busy professional, a student, or simply someone who values a healthy start to the day, overnight oats can become a staple in your morning routine. Enjoy the process of making them and delight in the flavors that greet you each morning. This simple dish not only nourishes your body but also simplifies your life, making healthy eating an effortless and enjoyable habit. For those who are always on the go, overnight oats can be a lifesaver. Imagine waking up, grabbing your jar of pre-prepared oats from the fridge, and heading out the door, knowing you have a wholesome meal waiting to be enjoyed. This convenience is particularly beneficial for those with hectic schedules, ensuring that a busy morning doesn't lead to skipping breakfast or making unhealthy choices.

5-Minute Pancakes

Waking up to the smell of fresh pancakes sizzling on the griddle is one of life's simple pleasures. However, the reality of busy mornings often means that this delightful breakfast is relegated to weekends or special occasions. But what if I told you that you could whip up a batch of delicious, fluffy pancakes in just five minutes? Yes, it's entirely possible, and all it takes is a bit of preparation and a foolproof method. Let's dive into the world of 5-minute pancakes and discover how to make them a staple in your morning routine.

The key to 5-minute pancakes lies in preparation and simplicity. By having your ingredients ready and using a quick, streamlined process, you can enjoy a stack of pancakes even on the busiest mornings. Begin by gathering your essential ingredients. For a basic pancake batter, you'll need flour, baking powder, a pinch of salt, sugar, milk, an egg, and a bit of melted butter or oil. These pantry staples come together to create a versatile batter that can be customized to your liking.

Start by mixing your dry ingredients. In a medium bowl, combine one cup of all-purpose flour, one tablespoon of sugar, one teaspoon of baking powder, and a pinch of salt. Whisk these together to ensure they are evenly distributed. This step can be done the night before and stored in an airtight container, making the morning preparation even quicker.

Next, move on to the wet ingredients. In another bowl, whisk together one cup of milk and one large egg until well blended. Add two tablespoons of melted butter or oil to the mixture, whisking continuously to incorporate. If you prefer, you can use buttermilk instead of regular milk for a tangier flavor and extra fluffiness.

Combining the wet and dry ingredients is where the magic happens. Pour the wet mixture into the dry ingredients, gently stirring until just combined. The key to fluffy pancakes is not overmixing the batter. A few lumps are perfectly fine and will disappear during cooking. Overmixing can lead to tough, chewy pancakes, which we definitely want to avoid.

With your batter ready, it's time to cook. Heat a non-stick skillet or griddle over medium heat. To test if the pan is hot enough, sprinkle a few drops of water on the surface. If they sizzle and evaporate quickly, the pan is ready. Lightly grease the pan with a small amount of butter or oil, using a paper towel to spread it evenly and remove any excess.

Using a 1/4 cup measuring cup, pour the batter onto the hot skillet, forming small circles. This size is perfect for even cooking and flipping. Cook the pancakes until bubbles begin to form on the surface and the edges look set, about 1-2 minutes. Flip the pancakes with a spatula and cook for another 1-2 minutes on the other side until golden brown. Repeat with the remaining batter, adding more butter or oil to the pan as needed.

While plain pancakes are delightful on their own, the beauty of this quick recipe is its adaptability. For a touch of sweetness, consider adding a handful of chocolate chips or blueberries to the batter before cooking. If you're in the mood for something savory, try mixing in shredded cheese and cooked bacon bits. The possibilities are endless, limited only by your imagination and pantry contents.

For those who enjoy a bit of a health boost, incorporating whole grains or alternative flours can be a great option. Whole wheat flour, oat flour, or almond flour can be used in place of or in combination with all-purpose flour. These flours add a nutty flavor and extra nutrients, making your pancakes not only quick and delicious but also nourishing.

Another time-saving tip is to make a large batch of pancake mix ahead of time. By combining the dry ingredients in bulk and storing them in an airtight container, you can have your pancake mix ready to go whenever you need it. When morning rolls around, simply scoop out the desired amount of mix, add the wet ingredients, and cook as usual. This method can significantly cut down on preparation time and ensure that you always have the makings of a quick breakfast on hand.

For those with dietary restrictions, this basic pancake recipe can be easily adapted. For a dairy-free version, substitute the milk with almond milk, soy milk, or any other plant-based milk. If you need an egg-free option, a flax egg (made by mixing one tablespoon of ground flaxseed with three tablespoons of water) works wonderfully. Gluten-free flour blends can replace all-purpose flour, allowing those with gluten sensitivities to enjoy pancakes without worry.

To make your 5-minute pancakes truly shine, consider serving them with a variety of toppings. Traditional options like maple syrup and butter are always a hit, but don't be afraid to get creative. Fresh fruits, yogurt, nuts, and even a dollop of whipped cream can turn a simple pancake breakfast into a gourmet experience. For a more indulgent twist, try spreading a layer of Nutella or peanut butter between two pancakes for a delicious pancake sandwich.

Another great way to enjoy pancakes is by making them into a pancake stack or pancake bar. If you have a few extra minutes, stack your pancakes with layers of fruit, yogurt, or even a drizzle of honey between each layer. This not only makes for a visually appealing breakfast but also adds a variety of flavors and textures to each bite. A pancake bar, with an array of toppings laid out, can be a fun and interactive breakfast option, especially for families or when entertaining guests.

In conclusion, 5-minute pancakes are a game-changer for anyone looking to enjoy a hearty breakfast without spending a lot of time in the kitchen. By preparing your ingredients in advance and using a simple, efficient method, you can whip up a batch of delicious pancakes in no time. Whether you stick with the classic recipe or get creative with mix-ins and toppings, these pancakes are sure to become a favorite in your household. Embrace the simplicity and versatility of this quick breakfast option, and start your day with a smile and a stack of pancakes. For those who enjoy experimenting with international flavors, there are countless ways to infuse global cuisine into your 5-minute pancakes. For a touch of French elegance, try making crepe-like pancakes by thinning out the batter with a bit more milk and cooking them in a larger pan. Serve these delicate pancakes with a sprinkle of powdered sugar and a squeeze of lemon juice, or fill them with fresh fruits and a dollop of crème fraiche.

Healthy Breakfast Bowls

A healthy breakfast bowl is more than just a meal; it's a vibrant start to your day that combines nutrition, flavor, and a touch of creativity. The beauty of breakfast bowls lies in their versatility, allowing you to tailor each one to your taste preferences and dietary needs. Whether you're rushing out the door or enjoying a leisurely morning, a well-constructed breakfast bowl can provide the energy and nutrients you need to tackle your day.

The foundation of any great breakfast bowl is a good balance of macronutrients: carbohydrates, proteins, and fats. Starting with a base that satisfies your carb needs is essential. Options like oatmeal, quinoa, or whole grain cereals provide a hearty and nutritious start. For a lighter option, consider yogurt or a smoothie base made from blended fruits and greens. Each of these choices offers a different texture and flavor profile, allowing you to mix things up throughout the week.

Oatmeal is a classic choice for a breakfast bowl base due to its fiber content and ability to keep you feeling full longer. Begin by cooking your oats according to package instructions. For added creaminess, use milk or a plant-based alternative instead of water. While the oats cook, you can prepare your toppings, making the process efficient and quick. Fresh fruits like berries, bananas, or apples add natural sweetness and a boost of vitamins. Nuts and seeds contribute healthy fats and a satisfying crunch, while a drizzle of honey or a sprinkle of cinnamon enhances the overall flavor.

Quinoa, often associated with lunch or dinner, makes an excellent breakfast bowl base as well. Rich in protein and essential amino acids, quinoa is a great option for those looking to increase their protein intake in the morning. Cook quinoa as you would for any other meal, then fluff with a fork. To give it a breakfast twist, consider adding a splash of almond milk and a dash of vanilla extract. Top with a mix of fruits, nuts, and perhaps a spoonful of Greek yogurt for creaminess and additional protein.

Yogurt-based bowls are a refreshing option, particularly during warmer months. Greek yogurt is a popular choice due to its thick texture and high protein content. For a dairy-free alternative, coconut or almond yogurt works well. Start by spooning your chosen yogurt into a bowl, then layer with a variety of toppings. Fresh berries, granola, and a drizzle of honey or maple syrup make for a delicious combination. If you prefer a bit more substance, adding a handful of chia seeds or flaxseeds can boost the fiber and omega-3 content.

Smoothie bowls are another fun and nutritious way to start the day. Unlike regular smoothies, smoothie bowls are thicker and meant to be eaten with a spoon. Begin by blending your favorite fruits, such as bananas, berries, and mango, with a small amount of liquid, like almond milk or coconut water. The goal is to create a thick, ice cream-like consistency. Pour the smoothie into a bowl and top with a colorful array of ingredients. Fresh fruits, nuts, seeds, and a sprinkle of granola add both texture and flavor. For an extra nutritional boost, consider adding a scoop of protein powder or a handful of spinach to the blend.

To create a truly balanced breakfast bowl, it's important to include a good source of protein. While yogurt and quinoa provide this naturally, other bases may require additional ingredients. Eggs, whether boiled, poached, or scrambled, are an excellent choice. They can be easily prepared and added to a bowl of roasted vegetables or whole grains for a savory twist. For plant-based protein, consider tofu or tempeh. Tofu scramble or marinated tempeh slices can be added to grain bowls for a satisfying and protein-rich option.

Healthy fats are another crucial component of a well-rounded breakfast bowl. Avocado, nuts, seeds, and nut butters are all excellent sources. Avocado can be sliced and added to savory bowls or blended into smoothies for creaminess. Nuts and seeds, such as almonds, walnuts, chia seeds, and flaxseeds, can be sprinkled on top of any bowl for added crunch and nutrition. Nut butters, like almond or peanut butter, can be drizzled over fruits or blended into the base for extra flavor and healthy fats.

Incorporating vegetables into your breakfast bowl is a great way to increase your daily intake of vitamins and minerals. While this might seem unconventional, many vegetables pair beautifully with traditional breakfast ingredients. Spinach, kale, and arugula can be added to smoothie bowls or sautéed and included in savory bowls. Roasted sweet potatoes, bell peppers, and zucchini provide a hearty addition to grain bowls. Tomatoes, cucumbers, and radishes add freshness and a bit of crunch.

One of the best aspects of breakfast bowls is their adaptability to different dietary needs and preferences. For those following a gluten-free diet, using gluten-free oats, quinoa, or buckwheat as a base ensures a safe and satisfying meal. Vegans can enjoy plant-based yogurts, tofu, and a variety of fruits and nuts. Those looking to reduce sugar intake can focus on using natural sweeteners like fresh fruit, cinnamon, and a touch of honey.

Preparation is key to making healthy breakfast bowls a regular part of your routine. Spending a bit of time on meal prep can make morning assembly quick and easy. Cook a batch of quinoa or oatmeal at the beginning of the week and store it in the refrigerator. Pre-wash and chop fruits and vegetables so they're ready to go. Having a variety of nuts, seeds, and other toppings on hand allows you to mix and match according to your mood.

For those extra busy mornings, overnight oats are a fantastic option. Combine oats with your choice of milk, yogurt, and any desired sweeteners or flavorings, then let it sit in the refrigerator overnight. In the morning, simply give it a stir and add your toppings. This make-ahead method ensures you have a nutritious breakfast ready with minimal effort.

Incorporating seasonal ingredients can keep your breakfast bowls fresh and exciting throughout the year. In the spring, fresh berries and tender greens are abundant and perfect for topping your bowls. Summer brings a variety of fruits like peaches, cherries, and melons, which add sweetness and juiciness. Fall is the time for apples, pears, and warming spices like cinnamon and nutmeg. Winter might be leaner in terms of fresh produce, but citrus fruits and hearty vegetables like sweet potatoes can still brighten your mornings.

Experimenting with global flavors can also add variety to your breakfast bowls. Try adding a dollop of tahini and a sprinkle of za'atar for a Middle Eastern twist, or coconut flakes and tropical fruits for a taste of the islands. A bit of curry powder and roasted chickpeas can lend an Indian flair, while soy sauce and sesame seeds can give a bowl an Asian-inspired flavor.

Ultimately, the best breakfast bowl is one that you enjoy and that fits your lifestyle. Whether you prefer sweet or savory, light or hearty, there's a combination out there that will start your day off right. By focusing on whole, nutrient-dense ingredients and taking a bit of time to prepare, you can create delicious and healthy breakfast bowls that fuel your body and delight your taste buds. Embrace the endless possibilities and make your mornings a little brighter with a beautiful, balanced breakfast bowl. The concept of breakfast bowls is not just about the ingredients; it's also about mindfulness and the joy of creating something nourishing. Taking a few moments each morning to assemble your bowl can be a calming ritual that sets a positive tone for the day. As you layer fresh fruits, crunchy nuts, and creamy yogurt or oats, you're not only crafting a meal but also investing in your well-being.

Grab-and-Go Muffins

Mornings can be a whirlwind of activity, with little time to prepare a nutritious breakfast. This is where grab-and-go muffins come in handy. These portable, delicious, and customizable muffins are perfect for busy mornings, ensuring you start your day with a healthy meal even when you're on the move.

The foundation of any good muffin is its base ingredients. Flour is a crucial component, and opting for whole grain or almond flour can boost the nutritional content. Whole grain flour, rich in fiber, helps maintain digestive health and provides a slow-release energy source, keeping you fuller for longer. Almond flour, on the other hand, is gluten-free and packed with protein, making it an excellent choice for those with gluten sensitivities or anyone looking to increase their protein intake.

Sweeteners are another essential element. Traditional muffins often rely on refined sugar, but healthier alternatives like honey, maple syrup, or coconut sugar can add sweetness without the detrimental effects of refined sugars. These natural sweeteners provide additional nutrients and have a lower glycemic index, which means they won't spike your blood sugar levels as dramatically.

The liquid ingredients in muffins also play a vital role in their texture and moisture. Milk is a common choice, but plant-based alternatives such as almond milk, oat milk, or coconut milk can be used to cater to dietary preferences or restrictions. These alternatives add unique flavors and nutritional benefits, with almond milk providing vitamin E and oat milk offering a creamy texture along with beta-glucan, a type of soluble fiber beneficial for heart health.

Eggs are another staple in traditional muffin recipes, providing structure and richness. For a vegan option, flax eggs (made by mixing ground flaxseed with water) or chia eggs (similar to flax eggs but using chia seeds) can be excellent substitutes. Both flax and chia seeds are high in omega-3 fatty acids, fiber, and protein, enhancing the nutritional profile of the muffins.

Incorporating fruits and vegetables into your muffins not only boosts their flavor but also their nutritional value. Fresh or dried fruits like blueberries, raspberries, apples, and bananas are popular choices. Blueberries and raspberries are antioxidant powerhouses, while apples provide fiber and bananas add natural sweetness and potassium. Vegetables like grated zucchini or carrots can be sneaked into the batter, adding moisture and a subtle sweetness while also increasing the fiber and vitamin content.

Nuts and seeds are perfect for adding texture and additional nutrients to your muffins. Chopped walnuts, almonds, or pecans introduce healthy fats and protein, making your muffins more satisfying. Seeds such as chia, flax, sunflower, or pumpkin seeds can add a crunch and are rich in omega-3 fatty acids, fiber, and minerals like magnesium and zinc.

Spices and flavorings are the final touch that can transform simple muffins into something extraordinary. Cinnamon, nutmeg, and vanilla extract are classic choices that add warmth and depth. For a more adventurous twist, consider adding cardamom, ginger, or even a hint of cayenne pepper. These spices not only enhance the flavor but also offer various health benefits, such as anti-inflammatory properties and improved digestion.

The process of making grab-and-go muffins is straightforward but requires some attention to detail. Start by preheating your oven and preparing your muffin tin with liners or a light coating of oil to prevent sticking. In a large bowl, mix your dry ingredients—flour, baking powder, spices, and any add-ins like nuts or seeds. In a separate bowl, whisk together your wet ingredients—eggs or egg substitutes, milk or milk alternatives, sweeteners, and any liquid flavorings like vanilla extract.

Combine the wet and dry ingredients gently, being careful not to overmix. Overmixing can lead to dense, tough muffins instead of the light and fluffy texture you're aiming for. Fold in any fruits or vegetables at this stage, distributing them evenly throughout the batter.

Fill your muffin cups about two-thirds full to allow room for the muffins to rise. Bake in the preheated oven until a toothpick inserted into the center of a muffin comes out clean, usually around 20-25 minutes depending on the recipe and oven. Let the muffins cool in the tin for a few minutes before transferring them to a wire rack to cool completely.

Once your muffins are baked and cooled, they can be stored in an airtight container at room temperature for a few days, or in the refrigerator for up to a week. For longer storage, consider freezing them. Simply place the muffins in a single layer on a baking sheet to freeze initially, then transfer them to a freezer-safe bag or container. This method prevents them from sticking together and makes it easy to grab one or two muffins as needed. Reheat frozen muffins in the microwave or an oven for a quick, warm breakfast.

Customization is one of the best aspects of making grab-and-go muffins. You can tailor them to your taste preferences or nutritional needs. If you're looking for a protein boost, consider adding a scoop of protein powder to the batter. For a lower-carb option, replace some of the flour with almond flour or another low-carb alternative. If you have a sweet tooth, adding dark chocolate chips or a swirl of nut butter can make your muffins feel like an indulgent treat while still being healthy.

For families, involving children in the muffin-making process can be a fun and educational activity. Kids can help measure ingredients, mix the batter, and choose their own add-ins. This not only teaches them about cooking and nutrition but also encourages them to enjoy healthier foods.

To make mornings even easier, consider preparing the dry ingredients for your muffins in advance. Measure out the flour, baking powder, spices, and any dry add-ins into a jar or container. When you're ready to bake, simply add the wet ingredients, mix, and bake. This small step can save valuable time during busy mornings.

Grab-and-go muffins are also perfect for sharing. Whether you're bringing them to a potluck, gifting them to a neighbor, or sharing with coworkers, homemade muffins are always appreciated. You can even package them individually in parchment paper or small bags for a thoughtful, convenient treat.

Incorporating grab-and-go muffins into your breakfast routine can simplify your mornings and ensure you're starting your day with a nutritious meal. By choosing wholesome ingredients and experimenting with flavors, you can create a variety of muffins that keep breakfast exciting and satisfying. Enjoy the process of baking and the benefits of having a healthy, delicious breakfast ready whenever you need it. Grab-and-go muffins are not only a practical breakfast solution but also a versatile snack option throughout the day. They can be enjoyed mid-morning, as an afternoon pick-me-up, or even as a pre- or post-workout snack. The portability and convenience they offer make them an excellent choice for anyone with a busy lifestyle, ensuring that you always have a nutritious option at hand.

Chapter 3

Simple Snacks and Appetizers

Fresh and Easy Dips

Dips are the unsung heroes of any gathering, offering a burst of flavor and a touch of elegance to snacks and meals alike. Fresh and easy dips are not only simple to prepare but also incredibly versatile, making them a must-have in your culinary repertoire. Whether you're hosting a party, packing a lunch, or simply looking for a healthy snack, a well-crafted dip can elevate your food experience.

The foundation of a great dip often starts with its base. Creamy bases such as Greek yogurt, sour cream, and cream cheese are popular choices due to their rich texture and ability to carry flavors well. Greek yogurt, in particular, is a fantastic option because it's high in protein and probiotics, which support digestive health. For a lighter alternative, consider using cottage cheese or pureed white beans; both provide a creamy texture without the extra calories and fat.

Avocado is another excellent base for dips, bringing its creamy texture and healthy fats to the table. A classic example is guacamole, which combines mashed avocado with lime juice, salt, and various add-ins like tomatoes, onions, and cilantro. The healthy fats in avocado are beneficial for heart health, and its fiber content helps keep you full.

For those who prefer a more vibrant base, consider roasted vegetables. Roasted red peppers, eggplant, or butternut squash can be pureed into smooth, flavorful dips. Roasting vegetables brings out their natural sweetness and adds a depth of flavor that's hard to achieve through other cooking methods. These bases are not only delicious but also packed with vitamins and antioxidants.

Flavor enhancers are what make each dip unique. Fresh herbs like parsley, cilantro, dill, and basil can brighten up any dip, adding freshness and a burst of color. Garlic and onions are also common additions, offering a pungent kick that complements creamy bases well. Roasting garlic before adding it to your dip can mellow its sharpness and add a subtle sweetness.

Spices are another way to bring complexity to your dips. Cumin, smoked paprika, and cayenne pepper can add warmth and depth, while a pinch of saffron or turmeric can introduce exotic flavors and vibrant colors. Don't be afraid to experiment with spice blends like za'atar, garam masala, or herbes de Provence to create unique flavor profiles.

Acidic components such as lemon juice, lime juice, or vinegar are essential in balancing the richness of creamy dips. They add a tangy brightness that cuts through the fat and enhances the other flavors. Citrus zest can also be a wonderful addition, providing a fragrant lift without the extra liquid.

Sweet elements can complement savory dips beautifully. A touch of honey, maple syrup, or agave can balance spicy or tangy flavors. For a more complex sweetness, consider adding caramelized onions or roasted sweet potatoes. These ingredients add a layer of depth and richness that's both unexpected and delightful.

Texture is another important aspect to consider. While smooth and creamy dips are delightful, adding some crunch can create a more interesting eating experience. Chopped nuts like almonds, walnuts, or pistachios can provide a satisfying crunch and additional flavor. Seeds such as sesame, sunflower, or pumpkin seeds can also add texture and nutrients.

Beans and legumes are fantastic for adding both texture and protein to your dips. Hummus, made from blended chickpeas, tahini, lemon juice, and garlic, is a classic example. It's creamy yet slightly grainy texture is a perfect vehicle for various flavors and can be topped with anything from olive oil and paprika to pine nuts and parsley.

Presentation plays a crucial role in making your dips appealing. Serving your dip in a beautiful bowl, garnished with fresh herbs, a drizzle of olive oil, or a sprinkle of spices can make a simple dip look gourmet. For added visual appeal, consider using colorful vegetables as dippers. Carrot sticks, cucumber slices, bell pepper strips, and cherry tomatoes not only add a rainbow of colors but also contribute to a healthier snack.

Pairing dips with the right dippers is essential. While chips and crackers are classic choices, fresh vegetables, whole-grain pita, or even fruit slices can offer a healthier and equally delicious alternative. For a more substantial snack, consider serving your dip with grilled chicken skewers, shrimp, or even roasted vegetables.

Dips can also serve as versatile components in meals. Use them as spreads in sandwiches and wraps, dollop them onto salads, or even stir them into pasta or grain bowls for added flavor and creaminess. A well-made dip can transform a mundane meal into something special with minimal effort.

For those with dietary restrictions, dips can be easily adapted to meet various needs. Dairy-free options can be made using coconut yogurt, cashew cream, or tahini. Gluten-free dips are naturally easy to achieve, especially when paired with gluten-free dippers like rice crackers or vegetable sticks. Nut-free alternatives can be created using seeds or legumes, ensuring that everyone can enjoy your creations.

Making dips ahead of time can save you valuable time, especially when entertaining. Most dips benefit from a few hours in the refrigerator, allowing the flavors to meld and develop. Store them in airtight containers to maintain freshness, and give them a good stir before serving. Dips can often be kept in the fridge for up to a week, making them perfect for meal prep and ready-to-eat snacks.

For a fun and interactive dining experience, consider setting up a dip bar at your next gathering. Offer a variety of dips and dippers, allowing guests to mix and match according to their preferences. This not only caters to different tastes but also encourages social interaction and culinary exploration.

Involving children in the dip-making process can be a great way to introduce them to new flavors and healthy eating habits. Let them choose their favorite ingredients, help with simple tasks like stirring or mashing, and taste-test along the way. This hands-on approach can make them more excited about trying new foods and eating healthy snacks.

Exploring global flavors through dips can be an exciting culinary adventure. From Middle Eastern hummus and baba ghanoush to Mexican guacamole and salsa, each culture offers unique and delicious dip options. Trying out different recipes can broaden your palate and introduce you to new ingredients and cooking techniques.

In conclusion, fresh and easy dips are a versatile, delicious, and healthy addition to any diet. By experimenting with different bases, flavor enhancers, and textures, you can create a wide variety of dips that suit your taste and dietary needs. Whether used as a snack, a meal component, or a party appetizer, dips offer endless possibilities for culinary creativity. Enjoy the process of making and sharing these delightful creations, and savor the joy they bring to your table. One of the greatest joys of making dips is the ability to customize them to suit your personal taste and dietary preferences. Experimentation can lead to delightful discoveries, and there's a certain satisfaction in creating a dip that perfectly matches your culinary vision.

No-Bake Energy Bites

No-bake energy bites are a simple yet powerful addition to any nutritional regimen, providing a quick and convenient source of energy and nutrients. These bite-sized snacks are perfect for busy individuals, athletes, and anyone needing a quick pick-me-up throughout the day. Creating no-bake energy bites involves combining wholesome ingredients that offer a balance of protein, healthy fats, and carbohydrates, making them both delicious and nourishing.

The foundation of most energy bites starts with a binding agent that holds all the ingredients together. Nut butters such as almond, peanut, or cashew butter are popular choices due to their rich flavor and creamy texture. They are also packed with protein and healthy fats, which help sustain energy levels. For those with nut allergies, sunflower seed butter or tahini can serve as excellent alternatives, providing a similar texture and nutritional profile.

Alongside the binding agent, a sweetener is often used to add flavor and help bind the mixture. Natural sweeteners like honey, maple syrup, or agave nectar are preferred for their subtle sweetness and additional nutrients. Honey, for instance, has natural antibacterial properties, while maple syrup contains antioxidants. These sweeteners also contribute to the chewy texture that makes energy bites so enjoyable.

Oats are a staple ingredient in no-bake energy bites, providing a hearty base that is rich in fiber and complex carbohydrates. Rolled oats are typically used for their texture, but quick oats can also work if you prefer a smoother consistency. Oats help to stabilize blood sugar levels, providing a steady release of energy that can keep you going throughout the day.

To boost the protein content, consider adding protein powder to your energy bites. Whether you choose whey, pea, or hemp protein, this addition can help repair muscles and keep you feeling full longer. Protein powder also blends seamlessly into the mixture, enhancing the nutritional value without altering the taste significantly.

Dried fruits add natural sweetness and a chewy texture to energy bites. Options like raisins, cranberries, apricots, or dates are packed with vitamins, minerals, and antioxidants. Dates, in particular, are often used as a natural sweetener and binder due to their sticky texture. Chopping the dried fruits into small pieces ensures they are evenly distributed throughout the mixture, providing a burst of flavor in every bite.

Seeds and nuts are excellent additions, offering crunch and a dose of healthy fats and protein. Chia seeds, flaxseeds, and hemp seeds are popular choices that also provide omega-3 fatty acids and fiber. Nuts like almonds, walnuts, and pecans can be chopped and mixed in for added texture and nutritional benefits. These ingredients not only enhance the flavor but also contribute to the overall satiety of the energy bites.

For those who enjoy a bit of indulgence, adding chocolate chips or cocoa nibs can satisfy sweet cravings while still keeping the snack relatively healthy. Dark chocolate, in particular, is rich in antioxidants and can provide a boost of energy. Opt for chocolate with a high cocoa content to maximize the health benefits while minimizing added sugars.

Spices can elevate the flavor profile of your energy bites. Cinnamon, nutmeg, and vanilla extract are commonly used to add warmth and depth. A pinch of sea salt can also enhance the overall taste by balancing the sweetness and bringing out the flavors of the other ingredients.

Making no-bake energy bites is straightforward and requires no special equipment—just a bowl, a spoon, and your hands. Start by combining the binding agent and sweetener, then mix in the oats, protein powder, dried fruits, seeds, nuts, and any additional flavors. The mixture should be thick and sticky but still easy to shape. If it's too dry, add a bit more of the binding agent or sweetener. If it's too wet, mix in more oats or protein powder.

Once the mixture is well-combined, use your hands to roll it into bite-sized balls. This process can be a fun activity to involve kids in, making it a great opportunity to teach them about healthy eating. Place the formed bites on a baking sheet lined with parchment paper, and refrigerate them for at least 30 minutes to help them firm up.

Storage is simple and convenient. Energy bites can be kept in an airtight container in the refrigerator for up to two weeks or frozen for up to three months. This makes them an excellent option for meal prep, ensuring you always have a healthy snack on hand. Simply grab a few bites from the fridge or freezer whenever you need a quick energy boost.

The versatility of no-bake energy bites means you can customize them to suit your taste preferences and dietary needs. For a tropical twist, try adding shredded coconut and dried pineapple. If you're a fan of classic flavors, a combination of peanut butter, oats, and chocolate chips can evoke the taste of a chocolate chip cookie dough. For those who prefer a more savory option, a touch of sea salt and roasted nuts can create a satisfying contrast to the sweetness.

Energy bites are not only a great snack but can also serve as a pre- or post-workout fuel. The balance of carbohydrates, protein, and fats provides the necessary nutrients to support physical activity and recovery. Consuming a couple of energy bites before a workout can give you the energy you need to perform, while having them afterward can help replenish glycogen stores and repair muscles.

In addition to being a convenient snack for busy adults, no-bake energy bites are also ideal for children's lunchboxes. They are a healthier alternative to store-bought snacks, which often contain added sugars and preservatives. Making energy bites at home allows you to control the ingredients and ensure they are both nutritious and delicious.

For those following specific diets, energy bites can be adapted to meet various dietary requirements. Gluten-free oats can be used for those with gluten intolerance, while vegan options can be made by using plant-based protein powders and sweeteners like maple syrup. Keto-friendly versions can be crafted using low-carb ingredients like almond flour, coconut flour, and sugar-free sweeteners.

Creating themed energy bites can add an element of fun and variety. Seasonal flavors like pumpkin spice in the fall or peppermint in the winter can make your energy bites festive and exciting. Experimenting with different combinations of ingredients keeps things interesting and prevents snack-time monotony.

In conclusion, no-bake energy bites are a versatile, nutritious, and easy-to-make snack that can fit into any lifestyle. By combining wholesome ingredients, you can create a delicious and satisfying treat that provides sustained energy and essential nutrients. The simplicity of the process, coupled with the ability to customize flavors and ingredients, makes energy bites a perfect addition to your culinary repertoire. Whether you're looking for a quick snack, a pre-workout boost, or a healthy option for your kids, no-bake energy bites are a delightful and practical solution. Incorporating no-bake energy bites into your daily routine can also encourage mindful eating habits. Taking a moment to savor these homemade snacks can transform a rushed snack break into a moment of pleasure and nourishment. The act of preparing these bites can be meditative and rewarding, fostering a deeper connection with the food you consume.

Homemade Hummus Variations

Hummus, a creamy and delicious spread made from chickpeas, tahini, lemon juice, and garlic, is a staple in many kitchens. Its versatility and nutritional benefits make it a popular choice for those seeking a healthy and satisfying snack. However, while traditional hummus is delightful, exploring different variations can introduce exciting flavors and textures to your culinary repertoire. Making homemade hummus allows you to customize it to your taste, experiment with new ingredients, and ensure the freshness and quality of your food.

The foundation of any hummus recipe starts with chickpeas. While canned chickpeas are convenient, using dried chickpeas can enhance the flavor and texture of your hummus. To prepare dried chickpeas, soak them overnight in plenty of water. The next day, drain and rinse them, then cook in fresh water until tender. This process may take an hour or more, but the result is a richer, creamier base for your hummus.

Tahini, a paste made from ground sesame seeds, is another essential ingredient. Its nutty flavor and smooth texture contribute to the classic taste of hummus. When selecting tahini, look for a high-quality brand with a smooth consistency and minimal separation. If you prefer a milder flavor, you can reduce the amount of tahini or substitute it with other nut or seed butters, such as almond butter or sunflower seed butter.

Lemon juice and garlic bring brightness and depth to hummus. Freshly squeezed lemon juice is always best, as it provides a vibrant acidity that balances the richness of the tahini. Adjust the amount of garlic to your liking; some prefer a subtle hint, while others enjoy a more pronounced garlic flavor. Roasting the garlic before adding it to the hummus can also mellow its sharpness and add a touch of sweetness.

Olive oil is often drizzled over hummus before serving, but incorporating it into the blend can create a smoother, more luscious texture. Choose a high-quality extra-virgin olive oil for the best flavor. Additionally, a pinch of salt is crucial to enhance all the flavors and bring the hummus together.

Once you have the basic hummus recipe down, you can start experimenting with various ingredients to create unique and delicious variations. Roasted red pepper hummus is a popular choice, adding a sweet, smoky flavor and vibrant color. To make it, roast red bell peppers until charred, peel off the skins, and blend the flesh into the hummus. A sprinkle of smoked paprika can enhance the smokiness and add a bit of heat.

Beet hummus is another visually stunning and nutritious variation. Roasted or steamed beets add a natural sweetness and earthy flavor, along with a brilliant pink hue. Simply blend cooked beets into the hummus and adjust the seasonings as needed. Beets are rich in antioxidants and vitamins, making this variation not only tasty but also healthful.

For a spicy kick, consider making jalapeño hummus. Fresh or pickled jalapeños can be blended into the hummus, along with a dash of cumin and lime juice for a southwestern twist. Adjust the amount of jalapeños based on your heat tolerance, and consider adding fresh cilantro for an extra burst of flavor.

Herb-infused hummus is a great way to incorporate fresh, vibrant flavors. Basil, parsley, cilantro, or dill can be blended into the hummus, either individually or in combination. Herb hummus pairs wonderfully with fresh vegetables and can also be used as a flavorful spread for sandwiches and wraps.

For a sweeter variation, try making sweet potato hummus. Roasted sweet potatoes add a creamy texture and natural sweetness that complements the savory elements of the hummus. This variation is particularly delicious with a touch of cinnamon or nutmeg and can be a delightful addition to a fall-inspired menu.

If you're looking for a protein boost, consider adding cooked lentils or edamame to your hummus. Lentils add a hearty texture and earthy flavor, while edamame brings a fresh, slightly sweet taste. Both options increase the protein content of your hummus, making it an even more satisfying snack.

Another intriguing variation is avocado hummus. Creamy avocados add a rich, buttery texture and a dose of healthy fats. This variation is especially delicious with a bit of lime juice and fresh cilantro, giving it a guacamole-like flavor that pairs well with tortilla chips or fresh veggies.

For those who enjoy a bit of sweetness and spice, carrot and harissa hummus is a fantastic option. Roasted carrots add a natural sweetness, while harissa paste brings a complex, spicy kick. This variation is perfect for those who enjoy bold flavors and can be a great addition to a mezze platter.

Experimenting with different spices can also transform your hummus. Adding curry powder, za'atar, or turmeric can introduce new and exciting flavors. A touch of ground cumin or coriander can add warmth, while a dash of cayenne pepper can bring heat. The possibilities are endless, allowing you to tailor your hummus to your specific taste preferences.

To make the process even more efficient, consider using a high-powered blender or food processor. This equipment ensures a smooth and creamy texture, especially when working with tougher ingredients like roasted beets or sweet potatoes. If your hummus is too thick, you can add a bit of water, olive oil, or aquafaba (the liquid from cooked chickpeas) to achieve the desired consistency.

Presentation also plays a key role in enjoying homemade hummus. Serve it in a shallow bowl, drizzled with olive oil and sprinkled with paprika, sesame seeds, or fresh herbs. Accompany it with an array of dippable items such as fresh vegetables, pita chips, or warm flatbreads. Hummus can also be a fantastic component of a larger spread, paired with olives, cheese, roasted vegetables, and other Mediterranean-inspired dishes.

In addition to being a delicious snack, homemade hummus variations can be a nutritious part of your diet. Chickpeas are a great source of plant-based protein and fiber, while tahini provides healthy fats and essential minerals like calcium and magnesium. By incorporating a variety of vegetables and herbs, you can boost the nutritional profile of your hummus even further.

Making hummus at home also allows you to control the ingredients, avoiding preservatives and excessive sodium often found in store-bought versions. You can adjust the flavors to suit your preferences and dietary needs, whether that means reducing the garlic for a milder taste or adding extra lemon juice for a tangier kick.

Sharing homemade hummus with friends and family can also be a rewarding experience. It's a versatile dish that appeals to a wide range of tastes and dietary preferences, making it a great option for gatherings and potlucks. Plus, the vibrant colors and flavors of different hummus variations can make your spread visually appealing and inviting.

In conclusion, homemade hummus variations offer endless possibilities for creating delicious, nutritious, and visually stunning snacks. By starting with a simple base and experimenting with different ingredients, you can discover new flavors and textures that keep your taste buds excited. Whether you prefer the smoky depth of roasted red pepper, the earthy sweetness of beets, or the spicy kick of jalapeños, there's a hummus variation to suit every palate. Making hummus at home not only allows you to customize it to your liking but also ensures that you're enjoying a fresh, wholesome, and satisfying snack. Integrating these homemade hummus variations into your weekly meal plan can lead to a more vibrant and enjoyable eating experience. They can be used in a plethora of ways beyond just a dip. For example, spread them on sandwiches or wraps for an extra layer of flavor and nutrition. They can be a fantastic addition to grain bowls, providing both protein and creaminess that complements grains like quinoa, farro, or brown rice.

Quick Bruschetta

Few appetizers capture the essence of fresh, simple, and delicious quite like bruschetta. Originating from Italy, bruschetta has become a beloved starter across the globe, appreciated for its versatility and the way it showcases the vibrant flavors of its ingredients. At its core, bruschetta features grilled bread rubbed with garlic and topped with a variety of ingredients, most commonly tomatoes and basil. However, the variations are endless, making it an ideal dish for experimentation and personal customization.

The foundation of any good bruschetta is the bread. Traditional Italian bruschetta uses a rustic, country-style bread with a firm texture that can hold up to grilling. A good choice is a loaf of ciabatta or a baguette, which offers a sturdy yet airy crumb. Slice the bread into pieces around half an inch thick. This thickness ensures that the bread becomes crispy on the outside while retaining a slight chewiness on the inside, providing the perfect canvas for your toppings.

Grilling the bread is a crucial step. It not only gives the bread its characteristic crunch but also infuses it with a smoky flavor that enhances the overall taste of the dish. You can grill the bread on an outdoor barbecue, a stovetop grill pan, or even under a broiler in your oven. Brush each side of the bread slices lightly with olive oil to help them crisp up and develop a golden-brown color. Once the bread is grilled, rub one side of each slice with a peeled garlic clove while the bread is still warm. The warmth of the bread helps to release the garlic's oils, imparting a subtle yet aromatic flavor.

The classic topping for bruschetta is a mixture of fresh tomatoes, basil, garlic, and olive oil. Start with ripe, juicy tomatoes. Roma or plum tomatoes are excellent choices due to their firm flesh and low water content, which helps prevent the topping from becoming too watery. Dice the tomatoes into small, even pieces and place them in a bowl. Add finely chopped fresh basil leaves, minced garlic, a drizzle of extra virgin olive oil, a splash of balsamic vinegar for acidity, and salt and pepper to taste. Let the mixture sit for a few minutes to allow the flavors to meld together. Before spooning the tomato mixture onto the bread, make sure to drain off any excess liquid to avoid soggy bruschetta.

While the classic tomato and basil bruschetta is always a crowd-pleaser, there are numerous other toppings you can explore to create exciting variations. One popular alternative is to use roasted red peppers. Roasting the peppers brings out their natural sweetness and adds a smoky depth to the dish. After roasting, peel the peppers and cut them into small strips. Combine with capers, chopped fresh parsley, and a splash of red wine vinegar for a flavorful topping.

For a more decadent option, consider a topping of creamy ricotta cheese with honey and figs. Spread a generous layer of ricotta on the grilled bread, then top with slices of fresh figs and a drizzle of honey. The combination of creamy, sweet, and slightly tangy flavors makes for an elegant and delicious appetizer.

Another delicious variation is mushroom bruschetta. Sauté a mix of mushrooms, such as cremini, shiitake, and oyster mushrooms, in olive oil with garlic and thyme until they are golden brown and fragrant. Finish with a splash of white wine or lemon juice to deglaze the pan and add a touch of acidity. Spoon the mushroom mixture onto the grilled bread and sprinkle with fresh parsley or grated Parmesan cheese for an added touch of flavor.

For those who enjoy seafood, a topping of shrimp and avocado offers a refreshing and satisfying option. Cook the shrimp in a skillet with garlic, chili flakes, and a squeeze of lemon juice. Dice a ripe avocado and toss it with the shrimp, adding chopped cilantro and a bit of lime zest for brightness. This topping pairs wonderfully with the crispy grilled bread, creating a delightful contrast in textures.

Prosciutto and melon is another classic Italian combination that translates beautifully to bruschetta. Thinly slice cantaloupe or honeydew melon and pair it with thin strips of prosciutto. The sweet, juicy melon complements the salty, savory prosciutto, creating a harmonious balance of flavors. For added depth, sprinkle with a few shavings of Parmesan cheese and a drizzle of balsamic reduction.

Vegetarian options abound as well. Consider a topping of roasted cherry tomatoes with goat cheese and herbs. Roast the cherry tomatoes with olive oil, garlic, and a sprinkle of salt until they burst and become caramelized. Spread a layer of creamy goat cheese on the grilled bread, then top with the roasted tomatoes and fresh thyme or rosemary. The tangy goat cheese and sweet tomatoes create a delightful combination that is sure to impress.

For a seasonal twist, try a topping of butternut squash and sage in the fall. Roast cubed butternut squash with olive oil, salt, and pepper until tender and caramelized. Toss with fresh sage leaves, a drizzle of honey, and a sprinkle of crushed red pepper flakes for a bit of heat. This topping brings a warm, comforting flavor to the bruschetta, making it perfect for cooler weather.

One of the joys of making bruschetta is the ability to tailor it to your personal taste and the ingredients you have on hand. Freshness is key, so always opt for the best quality ingredients you can find. Additionally, the simplicity of bruschetta allows the flavors of these ingredients to shine, so there's no need for overly complicated preparations or heavy seasonings.

Presentation is also an important aspect of bruschetta. Arrange the topped slices on a large platter, perhaps garnished with sprigs of fresh herbs or a scattering of edible flowers. The vibrant colors of the toppings against the golden-brown bread create an inviting and visually appealing dish that is sure to catch the eye of your guests.

Incorporating bruschetta into your entertaining repertoire offers a versatile and delicious way to start any meal. It can be served as an appetizer, a light lunch, or even as part of a larger antipasto spread. The variety of toppings allows you to cater to different tastes and dietary preferences, making it a crowd-pleaser for any occasion.

In conclusion, quick bruschetta offers a delightful combination of simplicity and sophistication. By starting with high-quality bread, grilling it to perfection, and experimenting with a range of fresh and flavorful toppings, you can create an array of delicious appetizers that celebrate the essence of Italian cuisine. Whether you stick with the classic tomato and basil or venture into more adventurous combinations, bruschetta is a dish that invites creativity and showcases the beauty of fresh ingredients. Enjoy the process of making and sharing this timeless appetizer, and let the flavors transport you and your guests to the sunny landscapes of Italy. The versatility of bruschetta extends beyond just the toppings and bread. It offers a unique opportunity to explore different textures and flavor profiles, making it a playground for both novice and experienced cooks alike.

Veggie and Cheese Platters

A well-curated veggie and cheese platter can transform any gathering into a memorable event. It's a versatile, crowd-pleasing option that combines the freshness of vegetables with the rich, complex flavors of various cheeses. Whether you're hosting a casual get-together or a formal dinner party, a thoughtfully arranged platter can serve as both an appetizer and a focal point for social interaction.

The first step in creating an impressive veggie and cheese platter is selecting the right ingredients. Fresh, high-quality vegetables and a variety of cheeses are essential. When choosing vegetables, aim for a mix of colors, textures, and flavors to create visual appeal and satisfy different taste preferences. Carrots, bell peppers, cherry tomatoes, cucumbers, radishes, and snap peas are excellent choices. These vegetables are not only vibrant but also provide a satisfying crunch that pairs well with the creaminess of cheese.

Cheese selection is equally important. A balanced platter typically includes a mix of soft, semi-soft, hard, and blue cheeses. Soft cheeses like brie or camembert offer a creamy texture and mild flavor, making them a favorite for many. Semi-soft cheeses such as gouda or havarti provide a smooth, buttery taste, while hard cheeses like cheddar, parmesan, or manchego add a robust, aged flavor. Blue cheeses, such as gorgonzola or roquefort, introduce a bold, tangy element that can be a delightful contrast to the other varieties.

To enhance the overall presentation and enjoyment, consider adding complementary items such as fresh fruits, nuts, and olives. Grapes, figs, and apple slices pair wonderfully with cheese, offering a sweet counterpoint to the savory flavors. Nuts like almonds, walnuts, and pistachios add an extra layer of texture and richness. Olives and pickles can introduce a briny, tangy dimension that balances the creaminess of the cheeses.

When arranging your platter, start by placing the cheeses first. This approach allows you to create a balanced layout and ensures that the cheeses remain the focal point. Cut some of the cheeses into slices or cubes, while leaving others whole with a knife for guests to cut as they wish. This variety not only makes it easier for guests to serve themselves but also adds visual interest to the platter.

Next, arrange the vegetables around the cheeses. Group similar colors together to create a cohesive look, and use contrasting colors to create visual pops. For example, place green cucumbers and snap peas next to red cherry tomatoes and bell peppers. This strategic placement makes the platter more inviting and easier to navigate.

Fill in any gaps with fruits, nuts, and olives. Scatter them evenly across the platter to ensure that every section offers a mix of flavors and textures. Adding small bowls or ramekins for items like olives, dips, or honey can also help keep the arrangement tidy and organized.

Consider including a variety of dips and spreads to complement the vegetables and cheeses. Hummus, baba ghanoush, and tzatziki are popular choices that pair well with most vegetables. A tangy mustard or a sweet fig jam can enhance the flavors of the cheeses. Offering a selection of dips not only adds variety but also allows guests to customize their bites according to their preferences.

Bread and crackers are essential accompaniments for a veggie and cheese platter. Choose a mix of options to cater to different tastes and dietary needs. Baguette slices, whole grain crackers, and gluten-free options ensure that everyone can find something they enjoy. Arrange the bread and crackers in a separate basket or on the edge of the platter to keep them from becoming soggy.

Temperature plays a crucial role in the enjoyment of cheese. Soft cheeses should be served at room temperature to allow their flavors and textures to fully develop, while hard cheeses can be served slightly cooler. Remove the cheeses from the refrigerator about an hour before serving to let them come to the ideal temperature. This step ensures that each cheese is at its best when your guests arrive.

Labeling the cheeses can be a thoughtful touch, especially if you're serving a variety of types. Small signs or labels can help guests identify each cheese and learn a bit about what they are tasting. This detail can also spark conversations and make the experience more interactive.

Pairing beverages with your veggie and cheese platter can elevate the experience. A selection of wines, beers, or non-alcoholic options like sparkling water or fruit juices can complement the flavors on the platter. For wine, consider offering both white and red options to suit different preferences. A crisp Sauvignon Blanc pairs well with fresh vegetables and creamy cheeses, while a robust red like Cabernet Sauvignon complements aged and hard cheeses.

For a more festive touch, consider creating themed veggie and cheese platters. A Mediterranean-themed platter might include feta cheese, olives, roasted red peppers, and pita bread, accompanied by tzatziki and hummus. An autumn-themed platter could feature seasonal vegetables like roasted butternut squash, along with aged cheddar, blue cheese, and a spiced apple chutney. Tailoring the ingredients to a specific theme or season can make your platter even more special and memorable.

Presentation is key to making your veggie and cheese platter inviting and appetizing. Use a large wooden board, a marble slab, or a decorative platter as the base. The natural textures and colors of these materials can enhance the visual appeal of the arrangement. Garnish the platter with fresh herbs like rosemary, thyme, or basil for an added touch of elegance and fragrance.

Lighting can also play a significant role in highlighting the beauty of your platter. Soft, warm lighting creates a cozy and inviting atmosphere, while natural daylight can make the colors of the vegetables and cheeses pop. Consider using candles or string lights to add ambiance to your setting, especially for evening gatherings.

As you create your veggie and cheese platter, remember that the goal is to delight and satisfy your guests. Pay attention to their preferences and dietary restrictions, and strive to offer a variety of options that cater to different tastes. The effort you put into selecting, arranging, and presenting the ingredients will be evident, and your guests will appreciate the thoughtfulness and care behind the platter.

In conclusion, a veggie and cheese platter is a versatile and elegant option for any occasion. By carefully selecting high-quality ingredients, arranging them thoughtfully, and adding complementary items, you can create a visually stunning and delicious centerpiece for your gathering. Whether you're hosting a casual get-together or a formal event, a well-curated platter offers something for everyone and encourages guests to mingle and enjoy the flavors together. Embrace the creativity and joy of assembling a veggie and cheese platter, and let it be a reflection of your hospitality and culinary enthusiasm. To further elevate your veggie and cheese platter, consider adding some homemade elements. Preparing dips, spreads, or pickled vegetables from scratch not only enhances the flavors but also adds a personal touch that guests will appreciate. For example, making a fresh herb dip with Greek yogurt, lemon juice, and a mix of dill, parsley, and chives can provide a zesty, refreshing complement to the vegetables. Similarly, creating your own pickled vegetables, such as radishes, carrots, or cucumbers, can introduce a tangy, crunchy element that is both unique and delicious.

Chapter 4

Effortless Lunches

Hearty Salads

Hearty salads offer a delightful combination of flavors, textures, and nutrients that can satisfy even the most discerning palates. These robust dishes go beyond the typical side salad, providing a substantial meal that can stand on its own. Whether you're looking to create a quick lunch, a dinner main course, or a side dish for a larger meal, understanding how to build a hearty salad is essential.

The foundation of any hearty salad is its base, which typically consists of greens. While iceberg lettuce might be the first thing that comes to mind, there are many more interesting and nutritious options to consider. Kale, spinach, arugula, and mixed baby greens each bring their own unique flavors and textures. Kale, for instance, offers a sturdy, slightly bitter leaf that holds up well to heavier toppings and dressings. Spinach provides a milder taste and tender texture, making it a versatile choice. Arugula adds a peppery kick, while mixed baby greens offer a variety of flavors and colors in one package.

Once you've selected your greens, it's time to think about the hearty components that will make your salad a meal. Protein is a key element, and there are numerous options to suit different dietary preferences. For a plant-based salad, consider legumes such as chickpeas, black beans, or lentils.

These not only add protein but also provide a satisfying texture and earthy flavor. Tofu and tempeh are other excellent plant-based proteins that can be marinated and grilled or sautéed for added flavor.

If you prefer animal-based proteins, grilled chicken, steak, or shrimp are all excellent choices. These proteins can be seasoned and cooked in advance, making meal prep easier and ensuring that your salad is both delicious and filling. Hard-boiled eggs and bacon crumbles can also add a rich, savory element to your salad, providing depth of flavor and additional protein.

Vegetables are the next crucial component of a hearty salad. Aim for a variety of colors and textures to keep things interesting. Roasted vegetables like sweet potatoes, beets, and Brussels sprouts add a caramelized sweetness and a tender texture that contrasts nicely with fresh greens. Raw vegetables, such as bell peppers, cucumbers, radishes, and cherry tomatoes, bring crunch and brightness. Including both roasted and raw vegetables ensures a dynamic eating experience with each bite.

Grains can also play a significant role in making your salad more substantial. Quinoa, farro, bulgur, and brown rice are all excellent choices that add bulk and heartiness. These grains can be cooked in advance and stored in the refrigerator, ready to be added to your salad as needed. They not only make the salad more filling but also contribute additional nutrients and a chewy texture.

Nuts and seeds are small but powerful additions that can elevate your salad. Almonds, walnuts, pecans, and sunflower seeds provide a satisfying crunch and a dose of healthy fats. Toasting them lightly enhances their flavor and adds a warm, nutty element to your salad. Additionally, seeds like chia, flax, and hemp can be sprinkled on top for an extra nutritional boost.

Cheese is another ingredient that can add richness and depth to your salad. Depending on your preference, you can choose from a variety of cheeses, such as feta, goat cheese, blue cheese, or parmesan. Each brings its own distinct flavor profile. Feta and goat cheese offer a tangy creaminess that pairs well with many vegetables, while blue cheese provides a bold, pungent kick. Parmesan, with its nutty and salty characteristics, can be shaved or grated over the top for a finishing touch.

Dressings are the final piece of the puzzle, tying all the ingredients together. A good dressing should enhance the flavors of the salad without overpowering them. Vinaigrettes made with olive oil, vinegar, mustard, and herbs are versatile and can be tailored to suit any salad. For a creamier option, consider dressings made with yogurt, tahini, or avocado. These can provide a luscious texture and a rich taste. When making your own dressing, always taste and adjust the seasoning to ensure it complements the salad perfectly.

Creating a hearty salad is not just about the ingredients but also about how they are prepared and combined. Start by ensuring that your greens are clean and dry, as excess water can dilute the flavors and make the salad soggy. Tossing the greens with a small amount of dressing before adding the other ingredients ensures that each leaf is evenly coated.

Layering the ingredients can also make a difference in how the salad is enjoyed. Begin with the greens, then add the grains, proteins, and vegetables. Finish with nuts, seeds, cheese, and a final drizzle of dressing. This approach ensures that each bite includes a variety of textures and flavors.

Serving your salad at the right temperature is crucial. While some components, like roasted vegetables or grains, may be served warm, the greens should remain crisp and cool. If you're preparing the salad in advance, keep the components separate and combine them just before serving to maintain the ideal texture and flavor.

Hearty salads are also a fantastic way to incorporate seasonal produce into your diet. In the spring, consider using tender asparagus, peas, and radishes. Summer offers an abundance of tomatoes, cucumbers, and bell peppers. Autumn is the perfect time for roasted root vegetables and hearty greens like kale. In the winter, look for sturdy greens and roasted squash or Brussels sprouts. By using seasonal ingredients, you not only enjoy the best flavors but also support local agriculture.

Experimentation is key to discovering new and exciting salad combinations. Don't be afraid to try different ingredients, dressings, and preparation methods. Mixing and matching allows you to find your own perfect balance of flavors and textures.

Incorporating international flavors can also add an interesting twist to your salads. A Mediterranean-inspired salad might include ingredients like olives, roasted red peppers, and feta, dressed with a lemon and oregano vinaigrette. An Asian-inspired salad could feature edamame, shredded carrots, and sesame seeds, with a soy-ginger dressing. Exploring different cuisines can keep your salad repertoire fresh and exciting.

Ultimately, hearty salads are a celebration of fresh, wholesome ingredients, thoughtfully combined to create a satisfying meal. They offer endless possibilities for creativity and customization, making them an ideal choice for any occasion. By focusing on quality ingredients and balancing flavors and textures, you can craft salads that are not only nourishing but also a joy to eat. Hearty salads also offer an opportunity to showcase your culinary skills and impress guests with visually stunning presentations. Consider the color palette and how the ingredients can be arranged to create an appealing look. For example, layering different shades of green with vibrant pops of red, yellow, and orange can make your salad visually enticing. Using a large, shallow bowl or a platter instead of a deep bowl allows each component to be seen and appreciated.

Simple Sandwiches and Wraps

Simple sandwiches and wraps offer a convenient, versatile, and delicious solution for meals on the go. They can be as straightforward or as elaborate as you desire, making them perfect for both novice cooks and seasoned chefs. The key to crafting an exceptional sandwich or wrap lies in balancing flavors, textures, and ingredients, ensuring every bite is a delightful experience.

A good sandwich starts with the bread. While traditional white or whole wheat loaves are classic choices, the world of bread offers many exciting options. Sourdough, rye, ciabatta, and focaccia each bring their own unique flavors and textures to the table. For a lighter option, consider whole grain wraps, tortillas, or flatbreads. The bread or wrap serves as the foundation, so choose one that complements the filling without overpowering it.

When it comes to fillings, the possibilities are endless. Proteins are a staple in most sandwiches and wraps, providing both substance and flavor. Deli meats like turkey, ham, and roast beef are popular choices, offering convenience and a familiar taste. For a more gourmet touch, consider using grilled chicken, sliced steak, or smoked salmon. These proteins can be prepared in advance and stored in the refrigerator, making meal prep a breeze.

Vegetarians and vegans can enjoy a variety of plant-based proteins. Chickpea salad, made with mashed chickpeas, lemon juice, and spices, mimics the texture of tuna salad and is equally satisfying. Grilled vegetables, such as zucchini, eggplant, and portobello mushrooms, add a hearty and flavorful element. Tofu and tempeh, when marinated and cooked properly, can also serve as excellent protein sources.

Cheese is another important component, adding creaminess and depth of flavor. Sliced cheddar, Swiss, and provolone are classic options, but don't be afraid to experiment with more unique varieties like brie, goat cheese, or blue cheese. For those avoiding dairy, plant-based cheeses made from nuts or soy can provide a similar texture and taste.

Vegetables bring freshness, crunch, and color to sandwiches and wraps. Lettuce, tomatoes, cucumbers, and bell peppers are common choices, but the variety doesn't end there. Consider adding shredded carrots, radishes, sprouts, or avocado for additional layers of texture and flavor. Pickled vegetables, such as pickles, jalapeños, or onions, can add a tangy contrast that brightens the overall taste.

Condiments and spreads are the final touch that can elevate a simple sandwich into something extraordinary. Mayonnaise, mustard, and ketchup are staples, but there are many other options to explore. Hummus, pesto, aioli, and tapenade each offer unique flavors that can complement and enhance your fillings. Experimenting with different combinations can lead to surprising and delightful results.

Assembling a sandwich or wrap is an art in itself. Start by spreading your chosen condiment evenly on the bread or wrap to ensure every bite is flavorful. Layering is key — begin with the protein, followed by cheese, then vegetables. This method helps to maintain the structural integrity of the sandwich, preventing it from becoming soggy or falling apart.

For wraps, it's important to not overfill them. Place the fillings in the center, fold in the sides, and then roll tightly from one end to the other. Using a piece of parchment paper or foil to wrap around the outside can help keep everything in place, especially if you're packing it to go.

Simple sandwiches and wraps can also be tailored to different cuisines, adding variety and excitement to your meals. A Mediterranean-inspired wrap might include hummus, falafel, cucumbers, tomatoes, and a drizzle of tzatziki sauce. An Italian sandwich could feature layers of prosciutto, mozzarella, roasted red peppers, and a splash of balsamic vinegar. Exploring different cultural flavors can keep your meals interesting and prevent monotony.

One of the great advantages of sandwiches and wraps is their portability. They make excellent options for picnics, road trips, or lunches at work. Preparing them ahead of time and storing them in airtight containers ensures they stay fresh and ready to enjoy. For added convenience, consider preparing a few different types at the beginning of the week to have a variety of options on hand.

Beyond their convenience and versatility, sandwiches and wraps can also be a healthy meal choice. By focusing on whole, unprocessed ingredients and incorporating plenty of vegetables, you can create a balanced and nutritious meal. Whole grain breads and wraps provide fiber and essential nutrients, while lean proteins and fresh vegetables contribute to overall health and wellness.

For those looking to reduce their carbohydrate intake, lettuce wraps offer a fantastic alternative. Large, sturdy leaves of romaine, butter lettuce, or collard greens can be used in place of traditional wraps. These options provide a fresh, crisp texture and can hold a variety of fillings. Lettuce wraps are particularly well-suited for Asian-inspired flavors, such as teriyaki chicken, sesame tofu, or spicy shrimp.

Kids can also enjoy simple sandwiches and wraps, making them a great choice for family meals. Involving children in the preparation process can encourage them to try new ingredients and develop healthy eating habits. Allowing them to choose their own fillings and assemble their own sandwiches can make mealtime fun and interactive.

When planning a party or gathering, consider offering a sandwich and wrap bar. Provide a selection of breads, proteins, cheeses, vegetables, and condiments, and let guests create their own custom creations. This not only caters to different tastes and dietary preferences but also adds a social and engaging element to your event.

For a touch of elegance, tea sandwiches are a charming option. These small, crustless sandwiches are typically filled with delicate ingredients like cucumber and cream cheese, smoked salmon, or egg salad. Cut into small, bite-sized pieces, they make a delightful addition to afternoon tea or a sophisticated luncheon.

Ultimately, the beauty of simple sandwiches and wraps lies in their adaptability and ease. With a few basic ingredients and a little creativity, you can craft delicious and satisfying meals that are perfect for any occasion. Whether you're looking for a quick lunch, a portable snack, or a crowd-pleasing party option, sandwiches and wraps offer endless possibilities.

In conclusion, mastering the art of simple sandwiches and wraps involves understanding the balance of flavors, textures, and ingredients. By selecting quality bread or wraps, incorporating a variety of proteins, cheeses, and vegetables, and experimenting with different condiments and spreads, you can create meals that are both delicious and nutritious. Whether enjoyed at home, on the go, or shared with friends and family, sandwiches and wraps are a versatile and delightful addition to any culinary repertoire. Don't forget the importance of proper storage to maintain the freshness of your sandwiches and wraps. If you're preparing them in advance, certain ingredients can be stored separately and assembled just before eating to prevent sogginess. For example, keep tomatoes, pickles, and other moisture-rich vegetables in separate containers and add them to your sandwich or wrap right before you eat. Using a dry, absorbent layer like lettuce or cheese can also help protect the bread or wrap from becoming too moist.

One-Pot Soups

One-pot soups are a culinary marvel, offering a comforting, nourishing, and convenient meal option. The beauty of these soups lies in their simplicity and the minimal cleanup required, making them an ideal choice for busy individuals and families alike. From hearty stews to delicate broths, the world of one-pot soups is vast and varied, promising both traditional favorites and innovative new creations.

The foundation of any great soup begins with the broth. Whether you choose a rich, homemade stock or a high-quality store-bought version, the broth sets the tone for the entire dish. Chicken, beef, vegetable, and seafood broths each bring distinct flavors and characteristics to your soup. Homemade broths are particularly rewarding, allowing you to control the seasoning and ingredients, ensuring a depth of flavor that is hard to match.

To create a homemade broth, start with a selection of bones, meat, or vegetables, depending on your preference. Simmer them with aromatics such as onions, carrots, celery, garlic, and herbs for several hours. This slow cooking process extracts the maximum flavor and nutrients, resulting in a broth that serves as a robust base for your soup. Strain the liquid to remove solids, and your homemade broth is ready to use.

Once you have your broth, the next step is to build the flavor profile of your soup. This often begins with sautéing aromatics like onions, garlic, and leeks in a bit of oil or butter. The gentle cooking of these ingredients releases their flavors, creating a fragrant base for your soup. Adding spices and herbs at this stage, such as thyme, bay leaves, or cumin, can further enhance the aroma and taste.

Proteins play a crucial role in many one-pot soups, adding both substance and flavor. Chicken, beef, pork, and seafood are popular choices, each imparting their unique qualities to the soup. For a classic chicken noodle soup, tender chunks of chicken simmer with vegetables and noodles in a savory broth. Beef can be used in hearty stews, such as a traditional beef barley soup, where the meat becomes melt-in-your-mouth tender after slow cooking. Seafood, like shrimp or fish, brings a light and fresh element, perfect for a Mediterranean-style soup.

Vegetarians and vegans have a plethora of options when it comes to one-pot soups. Legumes, such as lentils, chickpeas, and beans, provide a hearty and protein-rich base. Lentil soup, for instance, can be spiced with curry powder and coconut milk for a warming, aromatic dish. Chickpeas can be combined with tomatoes, spinach, and spices for a nourishing and flavorful soup. Even grains like quinoa or barley can add texture and nutrition, transforming a simple vegetable soup into a complete meal.

Vegetables are the soul of any good soup, bringing color, texture, and a wealth of nutrients. Root vegetables like carrots, potatoes, and parsnips add sweetness and body. Leafy greens, such as spinach, kale, and Swiss chard, contribute freshness and a vibrant green color. Seasonal vegetables can be highlighted, with butternut squash and pumpkin in the fall, or zucchini and tomatoes in the summer. The variety of vegetables available means you can create endless combinations, each with its own unique character.

One-pot soups also benefit from the addition of grains or pasta, which can turn a light soup into a filling meal. Rice, barley, farro, and quinoa each bring different textures and flavors. For example, a classic chicken and rice soup becomes creamy and comforting as the rice absorbs the broth. Barley adds a chewy texture to beef stews, while quinoa's light, fluffy texture is perfect for vegetable soups. Pasta, whether it's small shapes like orzo or larger ones like tortellini, absorbs the flavors of the broth and provides a satisfying bite.

The cooking method for one-pot soups is straightforward, making them accessible even to beginner cooks. After sautéing your aromatics and adding your spices, you simply add your broth, proteins, vegetables, and grains or pasta, then let everything simmer together until cooked through. This method allows the flavors to meld and develop, resulting in a harmonious and flavorful dish. The beauty of one-pot soups is their forgiving nature; you can often adjust seasonings and ingredients as you go, tailoring the soup to your taste.

One-pot soups are also incredibly adaptable to dietary needs and preferences. For those following a low-carb or keto diet, soups can be made with plenty of non-starchy vegetables and proteins, omitting grains and pasta. Dairy-free and gluten-free versions are easily achievable by selecting appropriate ingredients and broths. The flexibility of one-pot soups means you can create a delicious and satisfying meal that fits your lifestyle.

Serving and garnishing your soup can elevate it from a simple dish to a culinary experience. Fresh herbs like parsley, cilantro, or basil can add a burst of color and flavor when sprinkled on top just before serving. A squeeze of lemon or lime juice can brighten the flavors, while a dollop of yogurt or sour cream can add creaminess and richness. Crusty bread, homemade croutons, or a side salad can complement the soup, making for a complete and satisfying meal.

One-pot soups are also excellent for meal prep and leftovers. Many soups taste even better the next day, as the flavors continue to develop and meld. Soups can be stored in the refrigerator for several days or frozen for longer-term storage. Having a batch of homemade soup on hand means you always have a quick, nutritious meal ready to go, perfect for busy weeknights or lazy weekends.

Creating themed soups can add variety and excitement to your meals. A Mexican-inspired soup might include black beans, corn, tomatoes, and spices like cumin and chili powder, topped with avocado and fresh cilantro. An Italian-style soup could feature sausage, cannellini beans, kale, and a tomato-based broth, garnished with Parmesan cheese. Exploring different cuisines through soups allows you to experience a world of flavors and culinary traditions.

For those who enjoy entertaining, one-pot soups can be an excellent option for feeding a crowd. They are easy to prepare in large quantities and can be kept warm on the stove, ready for guests to serve themselves. A soup bar, with a variety of toppings and accompaniments, can add a fun and interactive element to your gathering, allowing guests to customize their bowls to their liking.

One-pot soups are a testament to the beauty of simple, wholesome cooking. With just a few ingredients and a single pot, you can create meals that are both delicious and nourishing. By focusing on high-quality ingredients and allowing the flavors to develop naturally, you can craft soups that satisfy both the body and the soul. Whether you're a novice cook or an experienced chef, one-pot soups offer endless possibilities for creativity and enjoyment in the kitchen. Exploring the possibilities of one-pot soups also means embracing the seasonal bounty available throughout the year. Each season brings its own array of fresh vegetables, herbs, and proteins, which can inspire new and exciting soup creations. In the spring, vibrant peas, tender asparagus, and fresh herbs like mint and dill can be combined to create a light and refreshing soup. A spring vegetable soup with a lemony broth and topped with a sprinkle of fresh herbs can evoke the essence of the season.

Quick Grain Bowls

Quick grain bowls are a versatile, nutritious, and satisfying meal option that can be tailored to suit any taste or dietary preference. They offer a balanced combination of grains, proteins, vegetables, and flavorful toppings, making them an ideal choice for busy individuals looking for a wholesome and convenient meal. The beauty of grain bowls lies in their adaptability and ease of preparation, allowing you to create a variety of delicious dishes with minimal effort.

The foundation of any grain bowl is, of course, the grain. There are numerous options to choose from, each bringing its own unique texture and flavor to the dish. Common choices include rice, quinoa, farro, bulgur, barley, and couscous. Quinoa, for example, is a protein-rich grain with a slightly nutty flavor and light, fluffy texture. It's perfect for those seeking a gluten-free option. Farro, an ancient grain with a chewy texture and nutty taste, adds heartiness to any bowl. Couscous, with its quick cooking time and light, fluffy texture, is ideal for those in a hurry.

Cooking grains is straightforward but requires attention to detail to achieve the perfect texture. Rinse grains like quinoa and rice to remove excess starch and bitterness. Use a ratio of one part grain to two parts water for most grains, though this can vary. Bring the water to a boil, add the grains, then reduce the heat to a simmer and cover the pot. Cooking times vary: quinoa typically takes around 15 minutes, while farro and barley may take up to 40 minutes. Once cooked, let the grains rest for a few minutes, then fluff them with a fork to separate the grains and enhance their texture.

Proteins are an essential component of grain bowls, providing the necessary sustenance and flavor. Options abound, from animal proteins like chicken, beef, pork, and fish to plant-based alternatives such as tofu, tempeh, beans, and lentils. Grilled chicken breast is a popular choice for its lean protein content and versatility. Marinate the chicken in a mixture of olive oil, lemon juice, garlic, and herbs, then grill until cooked through and juicy. For a vegetarian option, roast chickpeas in the oven with a drizzle of olive oil and a sprinkle of spices like cumin and paprika until they are crispy and flavorful.

Vegetables add color, texture, and a wealth of nutrients to grain bowls. Fresh, seasonal vegetables are always the best choice, offering the most flavor and nutritional value. Leafy greens like spinach, kale, and arugula provide a fresh, crisp base, while roasted vegetables like sweet potatoes, bell peppers, and Brussels sprouts add depth and sweetness. Raw vegetables such as cucumbers, cherry tomatoes, and radishes bring a refreshing crunch. To prepare roasted vegetables, toss them in olive oil, season with salt and pepper, and roast in a hot oven until tender and caramelized.

One of the keys to a delicious grain bowl is the dressing or sauce, which ties all the components together and adds a burst of flavor. There are countless options, from simple vinaigrettes to creamy dressings. A classic lemon-tahini dressing, made with tahini, lemon juice, garlic, and a touch of maple syrup, offers a creamy and tangy complement to grains and vegetables. A soy-ginger dressing, combining soy sauce, ginger, garlic, and a bit of honey, brings an Asian-inspired flair to your bowl. Experimenting with different dressings can transform the same basic ingredients into a completely new and exciting meal.

Toppings and garnishes add the finishing touches to grain bowls, elevating them from simple meals to culinary delights. Fresh herbs like cilantro, parsley, and basil provide a burst of freshness and color. Seeds and nuts, such as sunflower seeds, pumpkin seeds, and chopped almonds, add crunch and a boost of healthy fats. Avocado slices or a dollop of guacamole can add creaminess and richness. A sprinkle of feta cheese or crumbled goat cheese offers a tangy contrast to the other ingredients. Pickled vegetables, like red onions or cucumbers, bring a tangy brightness that cuts through the richness of the grains and proteins.

Building a grain bowl is an exercise in balance and creativity. Start with a base of cooked grains, then layer on your choice of protein and a variety of vegetables, both cooked and raw. Drizzle with your chosen dressing, then finish with a selection of toppings and garnishes. The possibilities are endless, allowing you to create a different bowl every time based on what you have on hand and what flavors you're craving.

For those who meal prep, grain bowls are a dream come true. Cook a large batch of grains at the beginning of the week and store them in the refrigerator. Similarly, prepare your proteins and roasted vegetables in advance, storing them in separate containers. When it's time to assemble your bowl, simply combine your prepped ingredients, add fresh vegetables and toppings, and dress as desired. This approach not only saves time but also ensures you have a healthy and satisfying meal ready to go whenever you need it.

Quick grain bowls are also perfect for accommodating different dietary needs and preferences. For a vegan option, skip the animal proteins and cheese, and load up on plant-based proteins like beans, lentils, and tofu. For a gluten-free bowl, choose grains like quinoa, rice, or gluten-free couscous. Paleo-friendly bowls can be created by focusing on grain-free bases like cauliflower rice or spiralized vegetables and incorporating plenty of proteins and healthy fats.

In addition to their practicality and versatility, grain bowls are an excellent way to introduce more whole grains, vegetables, and lean proteins into your diet.

They encourage mindful eating, allowing you to enjoy a variety of textures and flavors in each bite. As you experiment with different combinations, you'll discover new favorite ingredients and flavor profiles, keeping your meals exciting and satisfying.

Grain bowls are more than just a trend; they are a testament to the power of simple, wholesome ingredients combined thoughtfully and creatively. Whether you're looking for a quick lunch, a hearty dinner, or a meal prep solution, grain bowls offer a nutritious and delicious option that can be tailored to suit any taste or dietary preference. By focusing on high-quality ingredients and experimenting with different flavors and textures, you can create grain bowls that are not only quick and easy but also deeply satisfying and nourishing. One of the joys of making grain bowls is the opportunity to explore global cuisines and incorporate their unique flavors and ingredients. For instance, a Mediterranean-inspired grain bowl might feature a base of farro or quinoa, topped with grilled chicken, roasted red peppers, cucumbers, cherry tomatoes, and olives, all drizzled with a lemon-oregano vinaigrette and finished with a sprinkle of feta cheese and fresh parsley. This combination brings a refreshing and vibrant taste that transports you to the sunny coasts of the Mediterranean.

Light and Easy Pastas

Pasta is a beloved staple in many households, offering endless possibilities for creating light and easy meals that are both satisfying and delicious. When we think of pasta, rich and heavy dishes like lasagna or Alfredo might come to mind, but pasta can also be the foundation for fresh, light, and nutritious meals that take minimal time to prepare. From simple weeknight dinners to elegant dishes suitable for entertaining, light and easy pastas can fit into any occasion, providing comfort without the heaviness.

One of the keys to creating light pasta dishes is choosing the right type of pasta. While traditional semolina pasta is a great option, there are numerous varieties that can add different textures and flavors to your dishes. Whole wheat pasta, for example, offers a nutty flavor and a boost of fiber, making it a healthier alternative to regular pasta. For those looking to reduce carbs or increase vegetable intake, spiralized vegetable noodles, such as zucchini or sweet potato, can be a fantastic replacement or complement to traditional pasta.

Cooking pasta to the perfect al dente texture is crucial. This means the pasta should be firm to the bite but cooked through. Overcooking pasta can result in a mushy texture that detracts from the overall dish. To achieve al dente pasta, follow the package instructions carefully, but start checking doneness a minute or two earlier. Remember to salt the cooking water generously, as this will enhance the flavor of the pasta itself.

Now, let's explore some light and easy pasta dishes that can be whipped up in no time. One classic and simple recipe is Aglio e Olio, a traditional Italian dish that highlights the flavors of garlic and olive oil. Start by cooking your choice of pasta—spaghetti works particularly well. While the pasta cooks, heat a generous amount of extra-virgin olive oil in a large sauté pan over medium heat. Add thinly sliced garlic and cook until it's golden brown and fragrant, being careful not to let it burn. Toss the cooked pasta in the garlic oil, adding a pinch of red pepper flakes for a bit of heat. Finish with a sprinkle of freshly chopped parsley and a squeeze of lemon juice to brighten the flavors.

For a fresh and vibrant pasta dish, consider a Caprese Pasta Salad. This dish combines the classic flavors of a Caprese salad with the heartiness of pasta. Choose a short pasta shape like fusilli or penne, which will hold the dressing well. While the pasta cooks, prepare the other ingredients: halved cherry tomatoes, fresh mozzarella balls, and lots of fresh basil leaves. Once the pasta is cooked and cooled, toss it with the tomatoes, mozzarella, and basil. Dress the salad with a simple mixture of extra-virgin olive oil, balsamic vinegar, salt, and pepper. This light and refreshing pasta salad is perfect for a summer meal or a potluck gathering.

Another excellent option for a light pasta dish is a Lemon Herb Pasta with Grilled Chicken. This dish is both flavorful and satisfying, yet light enough for a warm evening. Start by marinating chicken breasts in a mixture of lemon juice, olive oil, garlic, and herbs such as thyme and rosemary. Grill the chicken until it's cooked through and has a nice char. Meanwhile, cook your pasta—linguine or fettuccine are good choices. In a large bowl, combine the cooked pasta with a generous amount of lemon zest, freshly squeezed lemon juice, and a drizzle of olive oil. Toss in chopped fresh herbs like parsley, basil, and chives. Slice the grilled chicken and serve it atop the pasta, with an extra sprinkle of herbs and a bit of grated Parmesan cheese.

Seafood also pairs beautifully with pasta for light and easy dishes. One such dish is Shrimp Scampi. For this recipe, you'll need a type of long pasta like spaghetti or linguine. Cook the pasta according to the package instructions. In a large skillet, melt butter with a bit of olive oil over medium heat. Add minced garlic and cook until fragrant. Toss in peeled and deveined shrimp, cooking just until they turn pink. Add a splash of white wine and freshly squeezed lemon juice, and let it simmer for a few minutes until the sauce slightly thickens. Toss the cooked pasta in the skillet with the shrimp and sauce, then finish with a sprinkle of chopped parsley and a pinch of red pepper flakes.

For a vegetarian option that's both hearty and light, try a Spring Vegetable Pasta. This dish is perfect when spring vegetables are at their peak. Cook a short pasta shape like farfalle or orecchiette. While the pasta cooks, sauté a mix of spring vegetables such as asparagus tips, peas, and artichoke hearts in a bit of olive oil. Add minced garlic and cook until the vegetables are tender but still crisp. Toss the cooked pasta with the vegetables, adding a bit of the pasta cooking water to create a light sauce. Finish with a generous amount of grated Pecorino Romano cheese and a handful of chopped fresh mint or basil.

Pasta doesn't always need to be served hot. Cold pasta dishes, like a Mediterranean Orzo Salad, can be incredibly refreshing. Cook orzo pasta and let it cool. Mix it with diced cucumbers, cherry tomatoes, Kalamata olives, red onion, and crumbled feta cheese. Dress the salad with a simple vinaigrette made from olive oil, lemon juice, minced garlic, oregano, salt, and pepper. This dish is perfect for a light lunch or as a side dish for grilled meats.

To keep pasta dishes light, it's also important to be mindful of portion sizes and the types of ingredients used. Using more vegetables and lean proteins like chicken or shrimp can bulk up the dish without adding excessive calories. Opting for olive oil instead of heavy cream-based sauces also helps keep the dish lighter and healthier.

Incorporating whole grains, fresh produce, and lean proteins into your pasta dishes not only makes them lighter but also adds nutritional value. Whole wheat pasta, for example, contains more fiber and nutrients compared to regular pasta. Fresh vegetables add vitamins, minerals, and antioxidants, while lean proteins provide essential amino acids.

Cooking pasta at home allows for endless creativity and customization. You can experiment with different ingredients, flavors, and textures to create dishes that suit your taste and dietary preferences. Whether you're looking for a quick weeknight meal or an elegant dish for a special occasion, light and easy pasta recipes offer a versatile and delicious solution.

By focusing on fresh, high-quality ingredients and simple preparation techniques, you can create pasta dishes that are both light and satisfying. These meals provide comfort and nourishment without the heaviness often associated with pasta. So next time you're in the mood for pasta, consider trying one of these light and easy recipes. You'll be surprised at how delicious and fulfilling a simple pasta dish can be. In addition to the recipes already discussed, incorporating seasonal produce can elevate your pasta dishes and keep them exciting throughout the year. For example, a Summer Vegetable Pasta Primavera is an ideal choice during the warmer months when fresh vegetables are abundant. Start by cooking a short pasta like penne or rotini. In a large skillet, heat olive oil and sauté a colorful mix of summer vegetables such as zucchini, bell peppers, cherry tomatoes, and corn kernels until they are tender. Add minced garlic and cook until fragrant. Toss the cooked pasta with the vegetables, adding a splash of white wine or vegetable broth to create a light sauce. Finish with fresh basil and a sprinkle of grated Parmesan cheese for a vibrant and flavorful dish.

9 798330 300747